The Irresistible Table

Mary DeMuth

DEDICATION

Of course this book is dedicated to my faithful taste-testers and all around amazing family. Patrick, you're still the best dessert chef there is, and your Christmas dinners have proven to be legendary. Sophie, I see you've caught the cooking bug, which forever ruins you for cafeteria food. Aidan, you're my bread inspiration. If I ever open a bakery, I know you'll stop by every day to grab a roll. Julia, I believe you'll be an amazing cook someday, perhaps even as a career. You'll have to learn to cook meat, though.

And to Pippin the Wonderdog, you are the funniest dog ever, and I'm convinced you spent your growing up years in a bakery. We'll always be buddies because I still delight in sneaking you hunks of bread.

Jesus, You're the reason I open my home and feed folks. Thank You for living a truly hospitable life.

CONTENTS

Introduction   i

1   Breakfast & Brunch   1

2   Appetizers   19

3   Salads   26

4   Pasta & Rice Dishes   38

5   Soups   51

6   Chicken, Fish and Meat   67

7   Veggies   91

8   Drinks   99

9   Bread   106

10   Desserts   118

INTRODUCTION

A survey by Kraft Foods Inc. and Yankelovich Partners in 2002 unearthed a surprising statistic: Seven in ten American families still sit down to dinner together at least five days a week. True to the "cocooning of America" phenomenon, people are spending more time in their homes together. The survey also noted that 89% of Americans say dinnertime is when family traditions are born. According to the Baylor college of medicine, meals eaten in community have 50% more fruits and vegetables than meals consumed alone.

The goal of *The Irresistible Table* is to give the home cook an arsenal of easy, delicious recipes and encourage a lifestyle of community and hospitality for her immediate community: her family. And the community she longs to gather around that family.

But doing so often involves a pesky word: hospitality. What is hospitality? In the dictionary, the word lies between hospital and host, an interesting juxtaposition. Our homes should be hospitals—places for our family and friends to recuperate and heal from the effects of this frenetic world. Our homes should also be incubators for up and coming hosts. Parents and children alike should learn the simple art of hosting others—in making them feel important, welcomed, and loved.

Perhaps you desire to have people over for dinner, to cultivate the art of hospitality with an eye toward community, but you don't know where to begin. Here are some suggestions as you get started.

Community is a celebration of others. When we invite people over, our goal is to help them feel special and appreciated. We want the mood of our home to be welcoming and comfortable so that our new friends feel at ease sitting on the couch or chatting with us in the kitchen. We listen to them and ask lots of open-ended questions. I dedicated an entire book to initiating conversations with the folks gracing our tables entitled *150 Quick Questions to Get Your Kids Talking*. Fostering this kind of open-listening approach grows community.

Community can be spontaneous. My husband Patrick and I have often invited people over for dinner on the fly, especially if I have made a particularly large pot of soup. These spontaneous dinners have been fun and casual.

We also enjoy hosting impromptu potlucks this way.

The time of day can be eclectic too. Why not have someone over for brunch, dessert, snacks, or a picnic at a park? Since we live in a world of busy evenings, we have found that often the only time people can come over is for a Saturday morning breakfast.

Community is an attitude. We've all been to dinners where there is such tension in the home that our presence seems like an intrusion; therefore, it is important to resolve spats before friends walk through the front door, or at least agree to work on conflict later.

The overarching attitude a good host possesses is other-centered service. Do unto your guests as you would like to have things done unto you if you were their guest. Take coats. Offer drinks. Ask if they are too hot or too cold.

Recently we had good friends over for dinner. I am always cold, even in Texas, so I was happy with our home's steamy temperature. When Patrick asked if they would like the fan on to cool things down, they nodded. Patrick thought of their comfort (while I donned a sweater!).

People like to feel like they are needed, so give them a task in the kitchen. Work alongside a friend as you ask casual questions. Offer appetizers if dinner will be late. Remember, you are welcoming community into your home. Your goal is to make your guests feel at home.

Community involves more than entertaining. It celebrates engagement. The word "entertainment" connotes that you must put on an elaborate show for someone—that every moment must be filled with activity and perfection. If your goal is simply to entertain someone, then your motivation is self-serving. You can become more interested in questions like *Is my pot roast OK? Is my conversation effective? Will they notice the stain on the carpet?*

Hospitality that is engaging is guest-centered. If your focus is there, you will ask questions like *Does she have any food allergies? What would he like to talk about? How can I help her to feel at home tonight?* See the subtle difference? Instead of putting on a show, hospitality with a heart bent toward community is all about putting others at ease.

With all these tips, remember that no one is perfect in their execution of hospitality. Mishaps happen. Roasts burn. Things are spilled. What people remember more is the way they felt in your home, not its spotless appearance or your perfect abilities.

Why I wrote this book

I'm not an expert cook. I have not graced the front page of *Food Network Magazine*. But I have cooked—a lot. Our family sits around the table almost every night of the year, eating meals I've concocted. What I am passionate about is amazing, easy-to-prepare food that blesses others. I've served folks around the world. I learned countless recipes through travel and living abroad in Southern France. I've fed five or fifty. And through it all, I've come to understand the importance of food and people, welcoming the beautiful synergy there.

Isn't it amazing that Jesus initiated His ministry around a wedding feast? And ended it around a Passover table? He turned bits and pieces into feasts of fish and bread. He told his fishermen disciples where to cast nets. He used food metaphors to describe our souls. Why? Because food is elemental. It's invitational. It's essential. And it brings people together.

That's my hope for you as you take these recipes into your community, that you'll see the holy privilege it is to gather friends with food. That your table will become as irresistible as Jesus Himself.

Chapter 1
BREAKFAST

I am a breakfast eater. I've tried (in vain) to convert my husband to my thinking. His idea of breakfast involves two strong shots of espresso with steamed skim milk. My children, however, are well on their way to becoming breakfast-loving adults, coffee notwithstanding.

Some of our most memorable times around the table involve breakfasts. With messy hair, wrinkled pajamas and beautiful (!) breath, we've enjoyed the casual camaraderie that comes from a relaxing breakfast. Often, we've invited friends over for Saturday breakfast—a great way to connect over muffins or eggs. To avoid a morning rush, I prepare muffin or coffeecake batter the night before, *and* I'm sure to tame my wild morning hair with a shower. No need in frightening the guests.

Crepes

I've been making these crepes nearly twenty years now. Forget the gimmicky crepe makers—all you need to make crepes successfully is a sturdy, non-stick pan and cooking spray. Our favorite way to eat them is Parisian style—rolled up with a smearing of Nutella inside. Raspberry jam and Nutella are also a great combination. Aidan eats them like pancakes, sliced into squares and topped with maple syrup. If you'd like to take this recipe and use it to fill crepes with meat or mushrooms, omit the sugar.

1 ½ cups flour
1 tsp. sugar
5 eggs
1 ½ cup milk
1/3 cup water
1 tsp. vanilla
3 Tbs. melted butter
cooking spray

In food processor or blender, add ingredients in order. Process 30 seconds until smooth. Pour into large measuring cup with a pouring spout. Heat heavy-bottomed non-stick frying pan over medium high heat. Spray with cooking spray. Pour a six-inch dollop of batter into the middle of the pan. Tilt the pan in a circular motion until the six-inch dollop spreads, creating a ten-inch crepe. When the sheen is gone and the crepe's surface bubbles have popped, flip over the crepe in one smooth motion with a non-metal spatula. Let cook 30-40 additional seconds. Place crepe on ovenproof plate and keep in a 250 degree oven. If your pan is heated up, each crepe should take no longer than a minute and a half. Repeat process until batter is spent. Place warmed crepes on table. Serve with fresh berries, whipped cream, Nutella, powdered sugar, maple syrup, or anything else your breakfast crowd desires. Makes 16 ten-inch crepes.

Note: Did you know that crepes sing? Once you've flipped them over, if you press down on them, you should hear a multi-pitched whistle emit from the hundreds of tiny holes. My children love to hear the crepes sing.

Berry Coffeecake

This coffeecake can be made the night before. Cover with plastic wrap and refrigerate overnight. In the morning, let it warm to room temperature, thirty minutes, before popping it into the oven.

2 large eggs
1 cup milk
2/3 cup white sugar
½ cup melted butter
1 tsp. vanilla
2 cups all purpose flour
1 Tbs. baking powder
1 cup frozen, loose-pack berries
1/3 cup softened butter
½ cup all purpose flour
½ cup oatmeal
½ cup walnuts or pecans
½ cup brown sugar

Preheat oven to 375. In large mixing bowl, beat eggs, milk, sugar, butter and vanilla until smooth. Add baking powder to the flour and stir through before adding both to the wet ingredients. Break apart berries and stir through. (If you stir too much, the berries will color the dough blue.) Spray an 11x13 baking pan with cooking spray. Spread coffeecake batter into pan.

In food processor, process butter, flour, oatmeal, nuts and sugar until just combined, using the pulse button. Top the coffeecake with the crumbled mixture. Bake for 35-40 minutes until a toothpick inserted in the middle comes out clean.

Substitutions: You may replace the berries with an equal amount of chocolate chips for a sweeter variation.

Ten Grain Hot Cereal

(You can find this in the hot cereal section or the organic section of your local grocery store. It looks like ground up grains and offers ten different grains. Or even yummier is steel cut oats. Prepare in the same way but cook for 25 minutes.)

1 1/2 cups boiling water
pinch salt
1/2 cup 10 grain cereal
handful of craisins (I buy mine at Costco)
1-2 tsp. brown sugar
handful of chopped almonds

Boil water in lidded saucepan. Add cereal and stir. Turn to low, cover, and simmer for ten minutes. Once done, add craisins, sugar and almonds.

Quick Tip: Did you know you can cook hot cereal in the microwave? Forget the ultra-sweetened packets from the grocery store. Instead, do this: Pour one part cereal (nine grain, oatmeal, etc.) to three parts water into a bowl at least twice as tall as the water level. (You don't want an oatmeal-lined microwave, so a big bowl is important.) For a single serving, this means 1/3 cup cereal to 1 cup water. Place the bowl in the microwave uncovered and cook on high for five minutes. Stir. Cook an additional minutes. Voila! Instant cereal without the expense and the sugar!

Broiled Grapefruit

We had something similar to this on our first anniversary at a bed and breakfast on Pender Island, part of the Gulf Islands in British Columbia. This is a great starter dish for a formal brunch.

5 grapefruits, cut in half horizontally
1 cup walnuts
1 cup brown sugar
1/3 cup butter
1 tsp. vanilla
¼ tsp. cinnamon

Preheat broiler. Cut around each triangle section of the grapefruit half so your guests won't have to dig! (There's nothing worse than squirting yourself or your neighbor in the eye with grapefruit juice!) In food processor, briefly process walnuts, sugar, butter, vanilla and cinnamon. Arrange grapefruits on a large jelly roll pan that has been sprayed with cooking spray. Top each grapefruit with crumbled mixture, pressing down to make sure it stays put. Broil until tops bubble and turn brown. Serve immediately. Makes ten.

Hearty Farmer's Omelet

This is easy to prepare and a crowd pleaser. To hurry the process, you can substitute frozen Potatoes O'Brien for the potatoes.

3 medium potatoes, cut into ½ cubes, skins on
¼ cup chopped green onion
3 Tbs. Butter
½ tsp. Cavendar's Greek Seasoning (or use your favorite seasoning salt to taste)
1 tsp. butter
5 eggs, beaten
salt and pepper to taste
3 Tbs. milk
¼ tsp. garlic powder
1 Tbs. parsley flakes
½ cup shredded cheddar cheese
½ cup cooked, cubed ham
1 cup shredded provolone, jack or mozzarella cheese

Place cubed potatoes in microwave-proof bowl and add ½ cup water. Cover with plastic wrap and microwave on high for 3 minutes until potatoes are tender. Pour potatoes into colander to drain excess water. Melt butter in large non-stick, ovenproof skillet. Add green onions, potatoes and seasoning and cook over medium high heat until browned evenly, about ten minutes. Place potatoes in bowl and cover with foil to keep warm.

Melt tsp. butter in potato pan. Whisk together eggs, salt and pepper, milk, garlic powder, parsley, cheddar and ham. Pour mixture into pan, cooking omelet style over medium heat. Poke holes in the egg mixture with a rubber spatula to ensure the top gets cooked. When the eggs are cooked, pour potatoes over the top. Top with cheese. Place pan under hot broiler until cheese is melted and bubbly. Serve in pie wedges. Serves four adults.

Pesto Garden Frittata

A frittata is an Italian omelet, served in wedges. Accompany this with seasoned, browned potatoes and a fruit salad.

2 medium zucchini, sliced into thin rounds
4 green onions, chopped
¼ cup shredded carrot
3 cloves garlic, pressed
1 Tbs. Olive oil
8 eggs
½ cup grated Parmesan cheese
½ tsp. salt
pepper to taste
2 heaping Tbs. Pesto (Pesto, a basil, pine-nut concoction, is now widely available in supermarkets and warehouse clubs.)
1 cup grated provolone or jack cheese
1 cup purchased marinara sauce

Using a non-stick twelve-inch frying pan, sauté zucchini, onion, carrots and garlic over medium high heat in olive oil until zucchini is slightly browned. Combine eggs, Parmesan, salt, pepper and pesto and pour over zucchini mixture. Cook until eggs are mostly done, with some liquid on top. Add cheese and broil top until cheese is melted and bubbly. Cut into wedges and serve from the pan. Top each wedge with warmed marinara sauce. Serves 4-6.

Mexican Strata

This is actually better if you make it the night before. Because you use day-old white bread, this is a thrifty entertainer's dream!

1/2 loaf day-old Italian or French bread, crusts removed, torn into pieces
2 7-ounce cans chopped mild green chilies
1 medium tomato, cut into ½ inch cubes
½ cup green onions, chopped
1 Tbs. Taco seasoning
½ tsp. salt
pepper to taste
1 tsp. Tabasco sauce
6 large eggs
1 ½ cups milk
2 cups grated cheddar or jack cheese

Spray a 9x13 pan with cooking spray and arrange torn bread over bottom until no pan is showing. In large bowl, combine chilies, tomato, onions, seasonings, Tabasco, eggs and milk until mixed through. Add 1 ½ cup of cheese. Pour over bread. Top with remaining ½ cup cheese and refrigerate overnight. Preheat oven to 350. Bake for one hour, until eggs are completely done. Serves 8.

To Die For Carrot Muffins

These muffins are moist, sweet, and satisfying. Serve with strong coffee and a fruit plate.

1 ½ cup peeled, shredded carrot
1 1/2 cups white sugar
1 Tbs. cinnamon
1 cup canola oil
3 eggs
1 tsp. vanilla extract
2 cups all-purpose flour
2 tsp. baking soda
1 tsp. salt
1 cup chopped walnuts

Preheat oven to 375. Place shredded carrot and ¼ cup water in microwave-proof bowl. Cover with plastic wrap and cook on high for three minutes. Drain the carrots and set aside to cool. In mixing bowl, combine sugar, cinnamon, oil, eggs and vanilla. Combine flour, salt and soda in separate bowl. Fold in flour mixture to egg mixture. Add carrots. Beat on medium high, 2 minutes. Fold in nuts.

Spray muffin tins with cooking spray. * Fill each cup ¾ full. Bake for 15-18 minutes. Makes 18 muffins.

I'm not a fan of paper muffin cup liners. When you serve muffins hot from the oven, the paper often sticks to a large portion of the muffin. If you wait for the muffin to cool, it works better. I like a bit of a crust on my muffins, however, where the fat in the muffin interacts with the metal of the pan. In my opinion, it makes a better muffin.

Dutch Babies

A hit with children and guests, these pancakes grow in the oven and puff up, Think of them as very large popovers.

4 large eggs
2 Tbs. sugar
1 tsp. vanilla
2/3 cup all purpose flour
2/3 cup milk
4 Tbs. butter

Preheat oven to 425. Beat eggs, vanilla and sugar until frothy. Add flour and milk and beat until well combined.

Melt 2 tablespoons each of butter in two large non-stick, ovenproof skillets. Tilt each pan until butter coats the entire surface. Add half of batter to each pan and pop them into different racks of your preheated oven. Bake for 15 minutes. When pancakes are slightly browned, turn on the broiler and broil each one until the tops are browned and puffy.

To serve, cut into wedges (four per baby). Serve with powdered sugar, preserves, Nutella, butter—anything your family or guests might want. Serves four. (This recipe can be easily doubled.)

Orange Walnut Scones

1 ½ cup all purpose flour
1 cup wheat flour
¼ cup ground walnuts (Use a small nut grinder or food processor.)
1/3 cup sugar
1 Tbs. Baking powder
½ tsp. salt
1 Tbs. Orange zest
½ cup butter
1/3 cup orange juice
1/3 cup milk

Preheat oven to 400. Combine the flours, walnuts, sugar, baking powder, salt and orange zest in large bowl. Using two knives or a pastry cutter, cut butter into mixture until it resembles fine crumbs. Add juice and milk and stir through with a wooden spoon until dough pulls away from the sides. Form dough into a ball. Dust the dough, a rolling pin and your work surface with flour. Gently roll the dough into a twelve-inch circle. Cut into eight pie-like sections. Transfer each scone to a well-greased baking sheet. Bake for 15 to 18 minutes until starting to brown. Serve with whipped cream, jam and butter. Makes 8 large scones.

Homemade Granola

My children love this breakfast granola. Store in an airtight container for up to three months in your pantry. You can also use it to top ice cream, muffin batter or yogurt.

10 cups rolled oats (I like the non-quick kind. Buy them in bulk in the bulk section of your grocery store.)
¾ cup chopped almonds
1 cup dry-roasted sunflower seeds
½ cup cornmeal
1 cup wheat bran
¼ cup sesame seeds
1 cup honey
½ cup brown sugar
1 cup peanut butter
1 tsp. salt
1 cup canola oil

Preheat oven to 225, yes that low. Combine oats, almonds, sunflower seeds, cornmeal, bran and sesame seeds in a very large bowl. In a medium saucepan over medium low heat, combine honey, brown sugar, peanut butter, salt and canola oil. Whisk until warm and mixed through. Pour peanut butter mixture over oats and stir through. Spray two large jelly roll pans with cooking spray and divide granola between them. Bake on two different racks for fifteen minutes. (Be sure to set your timer.) Stir. Alternate racks. Repeat process until granola is browned and crunchy, about one and a half hours. Makes 5 quarts.

Mary's Orange-Glazed Cinnamon Rolls

1 1/4 cup very warm water
1 packet yeast
1 Tbs. sugar
3 1/2 cups white flour
1 cup wheat flour
1/4 cup white sugar
1/4 cup melted butter
1/4 cup powdered milk
1/4 tsp. salt
1 egg

In clear container, combine water, yeast and sugar. Stir. Let sit five minutes until the top foams and is bubbly.

In large bowl, combine the remaining ingredients. Add yeast mixture. If you don't have a Kitchenaide, combine with a spoon and then knead five minutes. If you do, hooray!, just attach the dough hook and let it combine and knead the dough for five minutes. Spray bowl with cooking spray. Cover with plastic wrap and let stand one hour until double. Roll out dough into a long rectangle (probably 12 inches by 20 inches).

Pour 1/4 cup melted butter over the surface and spread evenly. Sprinkle cinnamon and sugar (you determine the amount) over that. Beginning from the long end, roll up the dough. To cut, use sewing thread. Move the thread under the dough, about an inch in, and then pull each end of the thread together. Place on greased cookie sheet. Cover with plastic wrap and keep cool (in the fridge) over night. Bake at 350 degrees for 25-30 minutes.

Glaze:

1 package cream cheese

1/4 cup orange juice
zest from one orange
1 tsp. vanilla
2 cups powdered sugar

Combine ingredients until smooth. Pour glaze over cinnamon rolls. Enjoy!

The Best Cream Scones Ever

I've made these for years now. This recipe is adapted from the Joy of Cooking.

2 cups all purpose flour
1/4 cup sugar
1 Tbs. baking powder (yes, tablespoon)
1/4 tsp. salt
1 1/4 cups heavy cream

Mix together the dry ingredients until combined. Add heavy cream and barely stir until mixed. Over-mixing will make them tough. Roll into an 8-10 inch circle and cut into eight pieces like a pie. Place each piece (apart from each other) on a greased baking sheet. Bake at 425 for 12-15 minutes. Makes 8. Serve with butter, jam, clotted cream (if you really want to be Britishy), and, of course, Earl Gray tea.

Très Vite Cinnamon Rolls

(For those of you who aren't très French, très vite means very fast)

5 Tbs. shortening or butter
3 cups flour
2 tsp. baking powder

Combine above ingredients by cutting with two knives until the shortening is in pea- sized crumbles.

1 cup milk

Combine milk and flour mixture with a wooden spoon until stiff, but don't over stir. Form into a ball. Flour a cutting board. Roll the ball into a 18x10 inch rectangle. Sprinkle the rectangle with:

1/2 cup sugar
1/4 cup melted butter
1 Tbs. cinnamon

Roll lengthwise (from one long end to the other long end.) Using a long thread of dental floss (not used!) slide the floss under the roll at one-inch intervals. Cross the floss over the top of the rolls and pull down like you are tying a shoe (this cuts it without having it compacted). Place each roll on a 9x13 greased pan. Bake at 375 for 20-25 minutes.

Cinnamon, Brown Sugar, and Chocolate Chip Coffee Cake

I had this at my sister's house. A friend of hers made it. Wow. I've modified the recipe.

1 cup butter
1 cup brown sugar
1 tsp vanilla
2 eggs
1 cup sour cream
2 cups flour
1 tsp. baking powder
½ tsp. baking soda
1 cup chocolate chips
brown sugar
cinnamon

Mix butter and sugar together, then add eggs and sour cream. Mix flour, powder and soda, then add to creamed mixture. Fold in and don't over mix. Spray a bundt pan with cooking spray. Sprinkle bottom with brown sugar and cinnamon. Add half of batter, then top with brown sugar and cinnamon and the chocolate chips. Add last half of batter, then sprinkle again with brown sugar and cinnamon. Bake at 350 degrees for one hour.

Orange Coffee Cake

1 cup butter
¾ cup sugar
2 eggs
1 cup sour cream or plain yogurt

2 cups flour
¼ tsp. salt
1 tsp baking soda
½ tsp baking powder
zest from one orange
½ cup orange juice

Cream together butter and sugar, add eggs and sour cream. Sift together dry ingredients and add them and the orange zest and juice to the bowl. Combine. Pour into bundt pan (well greased) and bake at 350 for one hour. Drizzle with glaze:

1 ½ cup powdered sugar
¼ cup orange juice.

Serve! Yum!

Chapter 2
APPETIZERS

My grandmother on my mom's side is the queen of appetizers. But not only does she make amazing little finger foods, she's the mistress of hospitality. She always makes sure you're not thirsty or cold or hot. She walks around her patio with little plates of goodness, offering food to everyone. She puts people at ease. I love this about her, and I hope to follow in her amazing footsteps.

My mom, too, is terrific at appetizers. She's not afraid to try new, exotic things, and she also loves to help others try their hand at creating little dishes. Once a caterer and food coach, she is inventive, but always a teacher.

When I was pregnant, all I craved was appetizers. I longed to eat small bits of loveliness, believing that if I did all my stomach woes would cease. And often they did.

Now when I entertain, one of my favorite things to do is invite people over for appetizers and desserts. They are easy to create. People like them. And they keep folks interacting with each other. They're also less intimidating to ask others to bring.

Think of appetizers this way, as a fun main dish with friends, or as teaser for what's to come. Either way, appetizers are fun, small, and typically easy to prepare.

Salsa

1/2 onion finely chopped
2 medium red tomatoes, chopped finely
2 medium yellow tomatoes, chopped finely (or just use all red tomatoes)
4 green onions, minced
2 cloves of garlic, pressed
Juice of 1/2 small lemon or lime
1/2 red bell pepper, chopped
1/4 cup well chopped cilantro
2 Tbs. chopped fresh oregano
1/4 cup red wine vinegar
1 tsp. paprika
Salt and pepper to taste
Hot sauce or chiles to taste

Place the onion and tomatoes in a bowl. Mash them slightly to create a little juice. Add all of remaining ingredients and stir through. Let mixture sit at room temperature for an hour, then serve or chill in refrigerator. Use as a dip for chips, or as an accompaniment to any Mexican dish.

Guacamole

2 large Haas avocados
Salt, pepper and garlic powder
3 dashes hot pepper sauce
2 Tbs. salsa
1 Tbs. sour cream
1 tsp. lime juice

Mash avocados, then season. Add hot sauce, salsa, sour cream, and lime. Serve immediately

Homemade tortilla chips

20 yellow corn tortillas
¼ cup peanut oil
Salt

This is the easiest, but one of the most rewarding appetizers. People love fresh chips! In stacks of five, cut tortillas into eighths until all tortillas are cut. (160 total triangles). Throw them on a cookie sheet, toss with oil, then salt to your taste. Bake in 400 degree oven for 15-20 minutes, stirring three times to make sure every one gets cooked. Serve with fresh salsa or guacamole.

Baked Brie with Raspberries and Nuts

1 wedge of brie or round of camembert (if you like a milder flavor)
1 cup raspberries (frozen is fine too)
1/3 cup brown sugar
½ cup chopped nuts of your choice

Grease small brownie pan (8 x 8) and place brie in the center. Top with berries, sugar and nuts. Bake for 15-20 minutes at 375. Serve with French bread rounds or really good crackers.

Baked Feta

When feta is cooked, something magical happens. It becomes creamy and amazing, and it grows milder.

1 hunk of feta (a little over a pound)
zest of one lemon
¼ cup lemon juice
¼ cup olive oil
Salt and pepper
2 cloves pressed garlic
¼ cup chopped fresh oregano (or 1 Tbs. dried)
Optional: chopped green olives, 2 Tbs. capers, ¼ cup roasted red peppers, 1/ 4 cup chopped walnuts.

Spray an 8x 8 cooking dish with cooking spray. Place feta in its center. Top with zest, lemon juice, olive oil, salt and pepper, garlic and oregano. Top with optional ingredients to taste. Bake at 375 degrees for 20-25 minutes until spreadable. Serve with pita chips.

Hot Gorgonzola Dip

My mom first made this for me. Serve with hunks of crusty Italian bread.

¼ cup butter
¼ cup flour

In a saucepan, heat butter until melted. Add flour and combine to form a roux.

1 cup chicken stock
1 cup milk
¼ cup cream
¼ cup white wine
1 cup crumbled gorgonzola cheese (or use blue cheese)
4 Tbs. grated parmesan
Salt and pepper to taste

Add the chicken stock, milk, cream and wine to the roux and stir until thickened, about ten minutes. Add cheeses and salt and pepper. To serve, pour dip into shallow long bowl and place in the center of a table. Serve alongside toasted bread. People simply grab a hunk, then dredge it in the dip.

Chapter 3
SALADS

My youngest daughter is a vegetarian. She watched all those food documentaries with me and came out on the other end happily munching on carrots and shunning the sinews. So she adores salads. She'd eat one every meal if she could, living up to her nickname, Bunny.

Salads tend to be forgotten, though. They're the last thing we think of after we've prepared a main dish, starch and veggie. We grab some triple washed greens (what a great invention), throw them in a bowl, and call it a salad. But there's so much more to the verdant lettuce head!

My favorite salad is the simplest one—arugula, shavings of parmesan cheese, good, ripe tomatoes, salt and pepper, a long squeeze of a lemon and olive oil. Another cheater dressing that is super close to the vinaigrette I loved when we lived in France involves dressing the salad in the moment. Throw a dash of balsamic vinegar, a few throws of olive oil, salt and pepper freshly milled, and a dollop of good old fashioned ranch dressing. Mix and serve.

And when summer's at its zenith, serve salad as a main course. Put out several bowls full of toppings and let folks create their own. Serve with freshly squeezed lemonade and a smile.

Apple/Spinach Salad

1 bunch of rinsed and torn spinach
1 large apple, cut into 1/2 inch cubes
1/4 cup sunflower seeds

Honey mustard dressing (recipe below)

1/4 cup honey
1/4 cup mustard
1/2 cup mayonnaise
1/4 cup rice wine vinegar
4 Tbs. water
4 Tbs salad oil (*Shake ingredients together until dressing becomes creamy*)

Be sure to rinse and re-rinse spinach. There is nothing worse than finding grit and dirt in a salad! Right before you are planning to serve the salad, cut the apple. (Or cut earlier and toss the apple with lemon juice to keep if from browning). Add sunflower seeds and toss with dressing. Serve!

Broccoli Pine Nut Salad

1 large head of broccoli, cut into very small pieces
1/2 cup pine nuts
3/4 cup halved red grapes
1/2 cup mayo
5 Tbs. red wine vinegar
2 Tbs. sugar

Toast the pine nuts by placing them in a nonstick pan and heating over medium until they turn brown (be sure to keep stirring them otherwise they will burn). Toss with broccoli. Add raisins. In another bowl, combine mayo, vinegar and sugar. Whisk until blended. Pour over salad. Serve. Makes 5-6 servings.

Chinese Noodle Salad

1/4 cup sesame oil
1/4 cup soy sauce
1 Tbs. Sugar
1 tsp. Chile oil
3 Tbs. Balsamic vinegar
1 pound spaghetti
1/4 cup toasted sesame seeds
1/2 cup green onions

Combine first five ingredients in bottom of salad bowl. Boil noodles until al dente. Run cool water over them until they're cold. Pour into salad bowl. Toss. Marinate several hours in the fridge. To serve: toss noodles again. Add sesame seeds and green onions. Toss again. Serves six. This is a great salad to bring to a potluck.

Mediterranean Pasta Salad with Olives and Capers

This side dish is a perfect contribution to any potluck picnic. Toss in a can of drained tuna for a more substantial salad.

¼ cup extra-virgin olive oil
2 Tbs. tomato paste
2 Tbs. balsamic vinegar
2 garlic cloves, minced
3 cups diced seeded plum tomatoes
2 cups chopped fresh fennel (about 1 medium bulb)
1 cup chopped fresh basil
6 green onions, chopped
½ cup chopped pitted Kalamata olives
¼ cup drained capers
16 ounces penne pasta

Whisk olive oil, tomato paste, vinegar, and garlic in a small bowl to blend. Season dressing with salt and pepper.
Combine tomatoes, fennel, basil, onions, olives, and capers in a large bowl. Sprinkle with salt and pepper. Let tomato mixture stand at least 30 minutes and up to 2 hours, tossing occasionally.

Cook penne in a large pot of boiling water until tender but still firm to bite, stirring occasionally. Drain pasta; rinse with cold water and drain again. Transfer pasta to large bowl. Pour dressing over and toss to coat. Add tomato mixture and toss to blend. Serves 12.

Simple Citrus Salad

1 large head bibb lettuce
2 oranges, peeled and cut into sections
18-24 asparagus spears cut into 2 inch sections, then steamed until tender then cooled.
¼ cup pepitos (toasted pumpkin seeds)

Toss above ingredients.

Citrus dressing:

Zest and juice from one lemon, lime and orange
1 chopped green onion
¼ cup white wine vinegar
¼ cup honey
½ cup canola oil
½ cup olive oil
3 Tbs. mayonnaise

Combine above ingredients in a blender. Dressing lasts for several days, and makes enough for three large salads.

Tomato/Mozzarella Salad

1 ball fresh mozzarella, cut into rounds, then cut in half (like half moons)
2-3 large tomatoes, ripe and yummy, sliced
1 bunch fresh basil julienned
2 cloves garlic, pressed
cracked pepper and sea salt to taste
¼ cup olive oil
Several dashes of balsamic vinegar

Arrange tomato slices and round half slices of mozzarella in a circular pattern on a large plate (alternate tomato and mozzarella). Top with slivered basil, garlic, salt and pepper. Drizzle olive oil over the top, then add several dashes of balsamic. Serve.

Italian Bread Salad

1 loaf good quality French bread
1/3 cup olive oil
4 pressed garlic cloves
Salt
4 large ripe tomatoes, chopped into 1 ½ inch dice
1/3 cup shaved parmesan. (Use a potato peeler to shave from a chunk of parmesan or romano cheese. If you don't have a hunk, you can use regular shredded parmesan)
½ cup chopped basil
Olive oil and balsamic vinegar

Cut French bread lengthwise. Pour olive oil onto baking sheet, then dredge the open end of each piece in the oil. Top with garlic and salt. Broil under broiler until brown. Let cool. Cut bread into 1 ½ inch cubes. Right before guests come, toss bread, tomato cubes, parmesan, and basil in large salad bowl. Drizzle salad with olive oil (about ¼ cup) and balsamic vinegar (about 7 dashes). Serve. Yum!

Cilantro Ranch Dressing

(great for taco salads or serving with tacos instead of sour cream)

1 cup mayonnaise
1/2 cup sour cream
salt and pepper
½ tsp. garlic powder
1 tsp. lime juice
¼ cup milk
1 tsp. sugar
1 can green chiles
½ cup chopped cilantro

Combine ingredients in a blender. Makes 2 cups of amazing dressing.

Rice Noodle Salad with Greens and Love

1 package rice cellophane noodles. (They are wide-ish and flat. You can find them in the Asian section of your grocery store.)

These are very quick to make. Boil a large pot of water and drop in the noodles. Reduce heat to medium and stir through until they're tender about 3-4 minutes. Pour into colander and rinse with cold water until the noodles are no longer hot.

Topping:

1 packaged ramen noodles
½ cup chopped almonds
¼ cup butter

Step on ramen noodles (still in package) until they're crushed. Add them and almonds to a sauce pan with butter and sauté until brown. This doesn't take very long, just a scant few minutes.

In four large bowls, add:

2 cups rinsed salad greens (8 total cups, divided among four bowls)
a fourth of the rice noodles
½ cup cubed meat (pork tenderloin, steak, chicken all work)
¼ cup each of carrots, celery, red peppers, chopped
The topping you made above divided into four parts

Dressing:

½ cup rice wine vinegar
½ cup vegetable oil
¼ cup sesame oil

¼ cup sweet hot sauce (found on the Asian aisle)
4 Tbs. soy sauce
¼ cup sugar

Combine in a lidded jar and shake until mixed. Pass the dressing with the salads. Makes four salads.

Barbecue Taco Salad

The magic of this salad is the dressing, and it's oh so easy to make and terribly yummy.

In a large salad bowl layer the following:

10 cups mixed greens
1 can black beans
1 can kidney beans
1 cup of cooked yellow corn (cooled)
1 ½ cup shredded cheddar cheese
1 cup chopped tomatoes
2 cups crushed tortilla chips

Dressing:

1 cup ranch dressing
1 cup barbecue sauce

Combine in a lidded jar and shake until ready. Before serving, toss the salad with the dressing. Even people who don't like salad love this salad.

Chapter 4
PASTA & RICE DISHES

Most of the pasta and rice dishes I've mastered have originated from me trying to duplicate amazing dishes I've had in restaurants and reworking recipes from cookbooks. To celebrate the latter, I'd like to share my absolute favorite cookbooks with you.

If I could, I'd buy every cookbook lining a bookstore shelf. Then I'd lock myself in my room with a pint of Ben and Jerry's and start reading. Mind you, I wouldn't start cooking, just reading (and wiping chunks of chunky monkey of my chin—or chubby hubby, or mint Oreo cookie).

That's the glory of cookbooks.

You can imagine the feasts you'd have. You can imagine the *Bon Appetit* crowd coming over to your immaculately appointed house with their yuppie sunglasses and their stories of safaris and PhD studies.

Eventually, though, my family pounds on the door to my locked room saying things like, "When is dinner?" or "I'm hungry, Mom." So, I extricate myself from the domineering pile of cookbooks and go about the art of creating food (usually pasta) for a family of five.

Really, though, I love to cook—that's why I love cookbooks so much. Below is my list of favorites and why:

The Joy of Cooking, by Rombauer, Becker & Becker. Everyone should have this updated staple of A to Z cooking. Whenever I need to know anything about food preparation, I flip through the almost 1200 page book. My favorite recipe in here is "Basic Muffins with milk or cream."

Since the dawn of time—well, actually since I tasted my first "Muffin Break" muffin—I've been searching for just the right muffin recipe. This recipe calls for ½ cup melted butter, which I'm sure is why the muffins are amazing. Soft, but not too sweet, and perfect with berries. And, by all means, do not use paper muffin cups. I've found that spraying non-stick muffin pans with cooking spray gives the muffins a wonderful skin. Plus, you don't miss any crumbs.

Better Homes and Gardens New Cookbook. This the red and white checkered cookbook you got for your wedding. Dust it off! I still get asked about my piecrusts. My secret? I use the cookbook's double crust pastry recipe on the inside front cover. Other favorites include: Beef barley soup, peanut butter cookies, poached eggs, and green goddess dressing.

Simply Classic. The Junior League of Seattle. Any time you see a Junior League cookbook at Half Price Books, pick it up. This one is amazing, with lots of regional specialties. The Northwest Autumn salad recipe is worth the price of the cookbook with its blend of apples, glazed pecans and crumbled blue cheese and a killer dressing.

Crust and Crumb, by Peter Reinhart. This book has done more for my bread making than any other. I used to pine over chewy, crusty Italian bread and wonder why I couldn't make it. This book taught me how, step by step. The most user-friendly part of the book is in the last chapter titled "The Bread Bakers Guild of America" where Reinhart shares his master formulas for baguettes and ciabatta, both of which are delicious.

Ina Garten Barefoot Contessa Family Style. My friend Suzanne Marinace, herself a great cook and a wonderful hostess, introduced me to the Barefoot Contessa cookbooks. Ina Garten's cookbooks are full of wonderful essays about hospitality and how to entertain in a casual, non-stressful way. Her recipes are simple and delicious. A must for anyone who wants good-tasting family-friendly food, and has a yearning to start entertaining. A shout out to my friend Stacey who also has all the Barefoot Contessa cookbooks.

The Crème de Colorado Cookbook. Another Junior league cookbook that is outstanding. The chocolate Indulgence dessert is one I make almost every time we have company. It's simple and velvety. Greek Lemon Chicken is something my friend Sue Harrell introduced me to, and then she gave me the cookbook. The spinach enchilada casserole is also really tasty.

Mark Bittman's *How to Cook Everything* is a cookbook that lives up to its name. It's a more modern approach to cooking and entertaining than *The Joy of Cooking,* but just as comprehensive and easy to follow.

The New Basics Cookbook by Rosso & Lukens is so loved, its pages are bent and dappled with food bits. I've made a lot of their soups—all tremendous. The chapter about risotto revolutionized the way I cooked rice. My friend Colleen introduced me to "Polenta, sausage, and tomato layers."

So next time you'd like to huddle up in your room reading cookbooks and eating Cherries Garcia, pick up one of these tomes. You won't be disappointed.

Chicken Spaghetti

1 whole rotisserie-cooked chicken

Strip the rotisserie chicken of most of its meat, leaving some. Place the remaining carcass in large pot of boiling water (8 cups water). Cook for 1 hour. Remove carcass. To the stock, add 8 cubes chicken bouillon (to taste) and stir through. Set aside on simmer.

In medium saucepan, add 2 Tbs. butter and melt over medium-low heat. Add 2 Tbs. flour and stir until combined. To this add:

1 ½ cups milk
1 ½ cups broth (from stock pot)
½ tsp. garlic powder
Salt and pepper to taste

Bring to a boil and stir until thickened. Turn off. Meanwhile, turn the chicken stock to high. When it's boiling, add 16 ounces spaghetti noodles. Boil for 10-12 minutes until al dente.

Turn on milk mixture while the noodles boil. Add:

2 cups cheddar cheese
1 small can mild green chili peppers

Stir through. When noodles are finished, drain and place in a large pasta bowl. Drop chicken pieces on top. Pour sauce over. Toss and serve. Serves a hungry family of five.

Stuffed Pasta Shells

1 package (12 ounce) jumbo pasta shells
4 cups ricotta cheese
1 cup shredded mozzarella cheese
1/2 cup grated parmesan cheese
2 eggs
1 Tbs. chicken food base (or granulated bouillon)
1/4 cup chopped fresh parsley
1 Tbs. dried basil
2 cloves garlic
1 cup chopped spinach, drained if frozen
pepper
1 1/2 cups spaghetti sauce (in a jar, or your own)
additional mozzarella and parmesan for the topping

Cook pasta according to package directions. Drain and cool. I keep mine in cold water until ready to assemble. Combine next ten ingredients in a bowl and mix well. Pour spaghetti sauce into large 9x 11 baking dish. Spoon a heaping large spoonful of the cheese mixture into each shell until it is overflowing. Put grated cheese over the top of the single layer of shells. Bake at 350 for 30 minutes. Broil the top if it is not browned and serve. Serves 6-8.

Spaghetti a la Homer

3/4 stick butter
2 garlic cloves smashed
salt and pepper to taste
1/4 cup fresh, chopped parsley
1/2 cup grated myzithra cheese (Find it in the specialty cheese case; it's Greek.)

Cook spaghetti according to package directions. Drain and place on four plates. Melt butter in saucepan. Add pressed garlic and salt and pepper. Stir butter constantly until brown. (It can burn, so make sure it only browns). Sprinkle cheese and parsley over noodles. Drizzle browned butter over the top. Makes four servings.

Sausage Spinach Pasta

2 cups chopped ripe tomatoes (or use canned)
1/3 cup capers with juice
4 cloves garlic, pressed
½ cup chopped fresh basil
1/3 cup olive oil
juice of one lemon
½ cup chopped fresh parsley
4 green onions chopped
sea salt and freshly ground pepper
1 pound Italian sausage
1 Tbs. Olive oil
1 bag fresh, cleaned spinach
16 ounces penne or bowtie pasta
1/3 cup freshly grated parmesan cheese

Combine tomatoes, capers, garlic, basil, olive oil, lemon juice, parsley and green onions in a large pasta bowl. Season with salt and pepper. Stir through. Let sit at room temperature 3-6 hours. Twenty minutes prior to dinner, boil salted pasta water. When you place the pasta in the water to boil, sauté sausage in olive oil until cooked through. The pasta and the sausage should be finished simultaneously. Drain pasta. Pour sausage and spinach into large pasta bowl with the tomato mixture. Pour hot pasta over top. Toss. Top with parmesan cheese. Serves 8.

Basmati Fried Rice

3 cups cooked basmati rice (leftover from the night before, cold)
2 tsp. Sesame oil
1 Tbs. Canola oil
1 ½ cup fresh spinach, chopped (triple washed from the grocery store)
2 Tbs. Oyster sauce
salt and pepper to taste

Heat oils in a wok or non stick skillet over medium high heat. Add rice and spinach and stir fry until rice begins to brown, and emits a nutty smell. Add oyster sauce and salt and pepper and heat through. Serves 4-6.

Mediterranean Salsa Pasta

2 cups finely chopped tomatoes
2 cloves pressed garlic (from jar)
4 green onions, chopped finely
2 Tbs. Capers
½ tsp. Sea salt
Dash of ground pepper
¼ cup olive oil
4 Tbs. Balsamic vinegar
15 Calamata olives, chopped, (Buy the pitted ones to save time.)

1 pound linguine
½ cup crumbled feta cheese

Combine first nine ingredients in a non-reactive bowl to make salsa. Cover with plastic and let marinate while you are at work. At dinner time, cook linguine according to package directions until al dente. Drain. Toss with salsa and feta cheese. Serves 6.

Lemon Shrimp Pasta

6 tablespoons butter
4 tablespoons olive oil
6 green onions, chopped finely
4 cloves garlic, pressed
30 shrimp, peeled and deveined
salt and pepper to taste
½ cup chopped Italian flat leaf parsley
zest of two lemons
½ cup lemon juice
½ cup grated parmesan cheese
16 ounces mini penne pasta

Put a large pot of water onto boil. When boiling, add pasta. While it's cooking (it should take ten minutes), sauté the onion and garlic in the butter/olive oil mixture, being careful not to let the garlic burn. Add the shrimp and cook until pink. Add salt, pepper, parsley, zest and lemon juice and combine. Simmer.

When pasta is finished, drain, then toss into the large saucepan with the shrimp. Cook through. Transfer to a serving dish, then top with grated parmesan. Serves 6.

Pan Fried Gnocchi

2 packages gnocchi (little Italian potato dumplings of goodness)
4 Tbs. butter
2 Tbs. olive oil
4 cloves of pressed garlic
salt and pepper
¼ cup chopped oregano (or you can use basil or sage)
Marinara sauce

Boil 4 quarts of water in large soup pot. When boiling, drop gnocchi in. It cooks very fast, and has a handy-dandy way of telling you it's done by popping to the surface. With a slotted spoon, remove surfaced gnocchi and place on paper towels to dry. Heat butter and olive oil in large skillet. Drop in the now-dried gnocchi into the pan. Add garlic, salt and pepper. Pan fry until gnocchi begins to brown (being careful that the garlic doesn't burn). Add oregano and stir fry until rendered, about 2 more minutes. Pour into a large pasta bowl. These are great as is, but then take on an even better dimension when topped with a great marinara sauce. (see next recipe).

Easy But Amazing Marinara

½ yellow onion chopped
3 cloves pressed garlic
2 Tbs. olive oil
1 can of tomato paste
2 cans chopped (not stewed) tomatoes
1/3 cup red wine
¼ cup chopped fresh basil
1 Tbs. brown sugar
salt and pepper to taste

Saute the onion and garlic in olive oil. Add can of tomato paste and stir until it starts to brown. This gives the marinara a smoky flavor and adds dimension. Add tomatoes, red win, basil, sugar and salt and pepper. Stir. Simmer for 15 minutes.

Lemon Barley "Risotto"

This is simply, amazingly delicious

1 tablespoon butter
1 tablespoon olive oil
1 red onion, chopped
2 heads garlic, smashed
1 cup pearl barley
zest from one lemon
2 cups chicken broth
¼ cup white wine

Saute onion in butter and olive oil until starting to brown. Add garlic and cook through, being careful not to let it burn. Add barley and sauté it until it looks brown and nutty. Add zest, broth and wine and bring to a boil. Turn to low, and cover the pot. Let simmer 35 minutes. Season to taste with salt and pepper.

Chapter 5
SOUPS

My first soups were watery and lacked flavor, the most memorable being a salmon soup where I used salmon bones to flavor the pathetically runny broth. The result was a reddish-hued fishy soup laced with tiny bones. Patrick, a wise newlywed, smiled and choked the stuff down.

My journey to create fabulous soups, obviously, started with a whimper. Through much trial and error, I've developed some surefire soup recipes—recipes that family and friends ask for regularly. Recently, Patrick told me, "You know, I think your soups are the best part of your cooking." It's proof that you can teach a young cook new tricks!

Tortilla Soup

My daughter Julia asks for this soup nearly every day. Patrick and I first tasted tortilla soup in Puerto Vallarta on our honeymoon. For several years, I looked for a recipe, gave up, and finally developed one of my own. If you don't have time to make the tortilla strips, you can substitute store-bought chips.

1 Tbs. butter
1 yellow onion, chopped finely
3 cloves garlic, pressed
1 small can green chilies
1 can (14.5 ounce) diced tomatoes
1 can black beans, drained (You may also use red kidney beans.)
1 cup frozen corn kernels
5 cups chicken stock
1 cup shredded chicken
1 Tbs. taco seasoning
salt and pepper to taste
12 yellow corn tortillas
¼ cup peanut oil
1 tsp. kosher salt
2 cups shredded jack cheese
Sour cream, for serving

Sauté onions and garlic in butter in a large soup pot over medium heat until onions are translucent. Add chilies, tomatoes, beans, corn, chicken stock, chicken and taco seasoning. Stir through on high heat until soup boils. Reduce to low. Add salt and pepper to taste. Simmer one hour.

With a sharp knife, cut tortillas into ¼ inch strips, stacking them four at a time to save time. Place all tortilla strips on a cookie sheet. Top with oil and salt. Toss the tortillas gently with your hands until they are all coated and the salt is evenly distributed. Spread in an even layer. Place in a 350 degree oven for thirty minutes until slightly brown and crisped. Remove and let cool.

To serve: Ladle soup into bowls. Top with a dollop of sour cream, a handful of jack cheese. Place a haystack of tortillas on top. Makes eight servings.

Fresh Tomato Basil Soup

This soup is especially lovely with homemade garlic-olive oil croutons and a dollop of crème fraiche or sour cream.

½ red onion, chopped finely
6 cloves garlic, pressed
1 Tbs. olive oil
4 cups fresh roma tomatoes, chopped (Or you can use two cans of canned, chopped plum tomatoes . . . just be sure they are uncooked, not stewed.)
1 ½ cup chicken broth
¼ cup chopped fresh basil
1 cup heavy cream
salt and pepper to taste

Sauté onion and garlic over medium heat in soup pot until onions are starting to brown, about five minutes. Add tomatoes, broth and basil. Cook over medium heat until tomatoes are cooked through, fifteen minutes. Add cream. Cool soup to room temperature. In batches, puree soup in blender. (To eliminate the cooling step, puree the hot soup with a hand held blender.) Return soup to pan and add salt and pepper to taste. Simmer on low until ready to serve. Serves four.

Chicken Corn Chowder

This is one of those cold-weather soups that children love as well as adults. Serve with cornbread sticks and a three-bean salad.

1 cup diced ham
2 Tbs. butter
1 red onion, chopped finely
2 Tbs. all-purpose flour
4 cups chicken stock
3 medium yukon gold potatoes, cut into one-inch dice
1 medium tomato, chopped finely
1 cup heavy cream
3 cups frozen corn kernels (Or cut kernels off three fresh cobs)
1 cup cooked chicken breast, torn
Salt and pepper to taste
¼ cup fresh parsley, minced

Place ham and butter in large soup pot and lightly sauté over medium heat, three minutes. Add onion and cook until onions are just starting to brown. Add flour and stir one minute over low heat, being careful not to burn the mixture. Pour in the stock and potatoes. Cook over medium heat for fifteen minutes, until the potatoes are tender. Stir in tomato, cream, corn and chicken breast. Adjust salt and pepper to taste. Cook on medium low heat for fifteen minutes. Add parsley, stir through, and serve. Makes 6 servings.

Apple Pumpkin Soup

1 medium-sized pumpkin, seeds removed and cut into 8ths
2 apples, cored and peeled and sliced
1 shallot, minced
1 tbs. olive oil
2 cloves garlic
5 cups chicken stock
1/2 cup white wine
Salt and pepper to taste
3/4 cup heavy cream

Cook pumpkin in 400 degree oven one hour until tender. Sauté apples, shallots and garlic in olive oil until shallots and apples begin to brown. Add baked pumpkin (scrape into soup, careful to not let any skin in), chicken stock and wine. Add salt and pepper. Cook 1 hour. Let cool. In batches, puree soup in blender. Return to pan. Add cream and stir until smooth. Serve with a dollop of crème fraiche, caramelized onions and roasted hazelnuts on top.

Clam Chowder

To save time and hassle, this recipe calls for canned clams. If possible, it's better to buy whole clams instead of chopped clams. Serve this chowder with a loaf of crusty sourdough bread and a tossed green salad. For a special presentation, purchase small sourdough rounds, hollow them out, bake them opened for twenty minutes at 350 and ladle soup into sourdough "bowls."

8 ounces bacon, fat removed as much as possible
2 Tbs. butter
1 ½ yellow onions, chopped finely
¼ cup flour
24 ounces canned whole clams (4 tuna-sized cans)
¼ cup water
6 medium red potatoes, cut into ½ inch cubes with peel
black pepper and salt to taste
4 cups milk
2 cups heavy cream
¼ cup fresh parsley, chopped

Cut bacon into ½ inch dice. Cook bacon in a deep soup pot over medium heat until crispy and slightly browned. Drain half the fat. Add butter and onions and sauté until onions are just starting to brown. Add flour, stirring constantly over low heat for 3-5 minutes. Drain the clam's juices into the soup pot and add ¼ cup water. Add potatoes, salt and pepper. Simmer on medium until the potatoes are tender—about ten minutes. Add canned clams and stir through. Pour in milk and heavy cream. Stir over medium heat until soup is warmed through. (Do not boil, or the soup will separate.) Add parsley right before serving. Adjust salt and pepper. Serves six.

Lentil Soup

This recipe, because it uses chicken broth instead of oil is low in fat and high in taste.

4 cups chicken broth*
1 large onion, chopped finely
1 cup sliced celery
2 cups sliced carrots (sliced into rounds)
1 14.5 ounce can Italian stewed tomatoes
1 tsp. dried basil
1 cup water
1 bay leaf
½ tsp. fennel
½ tsp. black pepper
1 cup rinsed lentils

In large soup pot on high, sauté the onions in ¼ cup of the broth until onion is slightly browned. Add remaining ingredients. Cover and bring to a boil. Turn heat to low and simmer until lentils are soft to bit, about one hour. Serves six.

*Note: Instead of paying high dollar for cans of chicken broth, purchase "real chicken base" from a warehouse club. Generally less than five dollars, you'll find it tucked away next to the spices. One container makes five gallons of MSG-free broth.

French Onion Soup

3 Tbs. butter
3 large yellow onions, sliced into rings. (To eliminate crying too much, slice in half and have your food processor cut them, using the slicer disk.)
1 bunch green onions, chopped
2 cloves garlic, pressed
2 Tbs. sugar
6 cups beef stock
1/3 cup red wine
Six pieces thick French bread
2 cups shredded Swiss cheese

In medium sized soup pot, sauté the onions, green onions and garlic in butter over medium heat for ten minutes. Add the sugar and stir constantly until the onions all turn brown. Be careful to stir the onions constantly at this stage. If you burn or scorch them, you have to start over. Add stock and simmer on low heat for forty-five minutes.

Meanwhile, place bread slices on a cookie sheet and bake at 250 degrees for forty minutes until they are hard. Add grated cheese and broil until cheese is melted and bubbly.

To serve, ladle soup into deep bowls. Just as your guests are sitting down for dinner, top the soup bowls with the cheese bread and serve. Serves six.

Black Bean Pumpkin Soup

Because of the pureed beans and the pumpkin, this soup can get thick if left on the stove too long. Before serving, thin soup with water to desired consistency.

1 can black beans, drained
1 15 ½ ounce can chopped tomatoes
1 large yellow onion, chopped finely
5 cloves garlic, pressed
3 Tbs. ground cumin
¼ cup butter
5 cups beef broth
1 large can pumpkin puree (Be sure you don't buy "Pumpkin Pie Filling," or you'll have
          a very sweet soup!)
½ cup white wine
1 cup diced ham
1 Tbs. balsamic vinegar
1 Tbs. red wine vinegar

In a blender or food processor, puree beans and tomatoes. In large soup pot, sauté onions, garlic and cumin in butter until onions are translucent and just starting to turn brown. Stir in bean mixture, broth, pumpkin and win. Simmer ½ hour over very low heat. Before serving, add ham and vinegars and stir through to heat. Add water if broth is getting to feel too much like pea soup. Pour soup into bowls. Garnish each serving with a dollop of sour cream and freshly minced parsley. Serves eight.

Cheese Vegetable Soup

My friend Diane introduced me to this easy-to-make soup. The best part of this soup is how quick it takes to make. In 30 minutes I can have homemade soup on the table.

¼ cup chopped onion
1 Tbs. butter
2 cups frozen corn
1 cup chopped fresh broccoli
¾ cup peeled and grated carrot. (Grate it like you would cheese in a cheese grater.)
½ cup water
2 10 ¾ ounce cans cream of potato soup
3 cups milk
1 cup shredded cheddar cheese
Salt and pepper to taste

In large soup pot, cook onion in butter until translucent. Add vegetables and water. Bring to a boil. Reduce heat and cover. Let simmer ten minutes. Stir in soup, milk and cheese and stir over medium low heat until cheese melts. Add salt and pepper to taste. Serves six.

Curried Cream of Carrot Soup

1 red onion, chopped finely
1 Tbs. olive oil
4 cups chicken stock
3 cloves garlic, pressed
4 cups peeled carrots, sliced into rounds
3 Tbs. curry powder
½ cup white wine
½ cup heavy cream
¼ cup fresh parsley, chopped
Salt and pepper to taste

Sauté onion in olive oil until onion is starting to brown. Add chicken stock, garlic, carrots, curry and wine. Bring to a boil, cooking until carrots are tender, ten minutes. Remove from heat. Use a hand-held blender to puree the soup. (Or let soup cool, and puree in batches in blender). Place soup back on the burner and warm over low heat. Add cream and parsley. Adjust seasonings, adding salt and pepper to taste. Serves six.

Beef Barley Soup

Nothing says comfort food to me like beef barley soup. This soup is easy to put together and is great accompanied by a dark brown bread.

1 yellow onion, chopped
1 Tbs. olive oil
3 cloves garlic, pressed
1 can chopped tomatoes
6 cups beef stock
1 1/2 cups shredded, cooked beef (Use leftover pot roast, brisket, or even steak, sliced thinly)
2 cups peeled and sliced carrots
1 cup sliced celery
½ tsp. each: basil, oregano, garlic powder
2 Tbs. dried parsley
2/3 cup barley (You can find barley in the dried bean section of your supermarket.)
 salt and pepper

Sauté onion over medium heat in soup pot until cooked through. Add garlic, tomatoes, beef stock, beef, carrots, celery, spices and barley. Simmer for 45 minutes. Add salt and pepper to taste. Serves eight.

Turkey Rice Soup from Scratch

One of the most important things to learn as a cook is how to make stock and soup from scratch.

½ turkey carcass with meat (or use one chicken or two game hen carcasses.)
Big stockpot
10 cups water
Leftover vegetables: onions, potatoes, peeled carrots, garlic, celery, anything you have on hand in the fridge. Just throw them in whole.
Salt and pepper to taste

Place all ingredients in the large stockpot and cover with plenty of water. Bring to a boil. Let simmer 2-3 hours. Place another stockpot in the sink. Pour soup contents through a colander into the other stockpot. Place stockpot back on the stove.*

When turkey carcass is cooled, pick through meat, tearing it into bite-sized pieces. To stock add:

Turkey meat
1 ½ cup chopped carrots
1 cup chopped celery or broccoli or leeks, whatever is on hand
½ cup chopped green onion
½ cup white wine
1 tbs. Garlic powder
2 Tbs. Real chicken base (or more if the soup lacks flavor)
2/3 cup brown or white rice
½ cup wild rice
1 cup milk
¼ cup fresh chopped parsley

Let simmer one hour. You can also let this simmer all day—it fills the house with soup bouquet! Serves 10-12

*A better way to do this is to use your pasta insert for your stockpot. A pasta insert nests inside a stockpot nicely. When the stock is finished, simply lift the pasta insert (It has holes) out of the pot. The carcass and vegetables will stay in the pasta insert, leaving the broth behind in the stockpot.

Note: Anytime you have a leftover turkey, game hen, or chicken carcass, store it in the freezer in a zippered freezer bag. When you have carrot ends, bits of lettuce, onion peels, etc, add those to the bag. When the bag's full, dump the entire contents into a pot of water, add salt and let the whole thing percolate for several hours. Once you remove everything, voila! You have stock. You can freeze stock in ice cube trays, and then in zippered freezer bags. That way, you'll always have some homemade stock on hand.

A Different Kind of Chicken Noodle Soup *(easy!)*

My friend D'Ann made a rendition of this that was amazing. I've tweaked it a bit.

4 green onions, chopped
olive oil
6 cups chicken broth
4 cups raw spinach
1 ½ cup orzo pasta
10-12 meatballs (turkey) or fully cooked chicken sausage cut up (about 2 cups)

Sauté green onions in large soup pan until wilted. Add chicken broth to pan, then the next 3 ingredients. Bring to a boil. Cook until orzo is tender, 9 minutes.

Chapter 6
CHICKEN, FISH, AND MEAT

When I first started cooking, meat mystified me. Pasta sauces and chicken breasts I could master without too much fanfare, but it took me many years how to cook different cuts of meat. My first roasts either resembled bloody battle scenes or old, dry shoes.

My favorite way of cooking, now, is marinating and grilling. I like the tanginess of the marinade married with the smokiness of the barbecue. Slow cooked meats, however, are very good too, and they contribute to new dishes the next week. The following are my favorite and foolproof meat recipes.

Crockpot Moroccan Chicken

2 Tbs. olive oil
1 whole chicken, cut up (or more if you have a bigger family), skin off
1 onion, chopped
2 Tbs. ras el hanout spice mix (or you can use really good curry powder)
a few saffron threads
1 cup chicken stock
1 can chopped tomatoes
2 cups dried halved apricots
1 tablespoon honey
1/4 cup orange juice
salt and pepper

Saute onions and chicken in skillet in olive oil until browned. Add to crockpot. Add everything else, stir and cook on low for the day. Serve with rice or cous cous.

Rolled Stuffed Pork Loin

Guests will think you worked hard on this one. Be sure to throw some flour on your face to accomplish the deception.

1 3-5 pound pork loin roast
¾ cup pitted prunes (or you can substitute ½ cup dried cranberries)
¼ cup red wine
¼ cup walnuts, pine nuts, pecans, or hazelnuts
½ apple, cored and cute into cubes
4 Tbs. Dijon mustard

To prepare roast: With a sharp knife, cut roast into one long, wide strip as if you are uncoiling a cinnamon roll. The initial incision should be one inch thick. The roast will lay flat when you are finished.

Place prunes, wine, nuts and apple in food processor and process until smooth, 30 seconds. (If you don't have a processor, chop the prunes, nuts and apples by hand, place in a bowl and stir wine through.)

Spread stuffing over roast and roll it back onto itself, securing with butcher's string (or any non-hairy string . . . Yarn doesn't work!) Spread Dijon mustard over top and sides of secured roast.

Place roast in a roasting pan that has been slightly greased with olive oil. Bake at 325 degrees for 1-½ hours or until the internal temperature reaches 170 degrees. A five pound roast will take ½ hour longer. Slice vertically to show the roulade of the meat and fruit.

Crockpot Sweet and Sour Pork Chops

In bottom of crockpot, add:

1/2 chopped onion
4 stalks celery, chopped
5 green onions, chopped
1 red bell pepper, chopped
2 cloves garlic, pressed
1/2 tsp. fresh ginger
1/4 cup soy sauce
1/4 cup red wine vinegar
1/2 cup chicken stock
4 Tbs. ketchup
1/4 4 cup sugar
1 Tbs. sesame oil

Stir together.

Add 4-8 pork chops and toss to coat. Cook all day. Serve with stir fried veggies and rice.

Chicken Artichoke Heart Casserole

4 whole chicken breasts
1 14 ounce can artichoke hearts, drained
1/3 cup butter (I will use less)
1/3 cup flour (I will use less, more like 1/4 cup)
2 1/2 cups chicken broth
1/4 cup white wine
4 cups shredded cheddar cheese
2 Tbsp. green onions
1/4 cup Parmesan cheese, grated
1 cup bread crumbs

Sauté chicken breasts in a little olive oil until done. Cut into large chunks. Layer chicken and artichokes in a 9x13 pan. Melt butter in medium sauce pan, add flour to create a roux. Add chicken broth and stir until thickened and combined. Add wine and cheddar and onions over low heat. Stir until melted. Pour sauce over casserole. Combine bread crumbs and Parmesan and sprinkle over casserole. Bake uncovered at 350 degrees for 25 minutes. Serve with rice or pasta.

Salmon Cakes with Sweet Hot Sauce

2 eight ounce cans salmon
2 eggs
2/3 cup packaged bread crumbs
A dash of Worcestershire sauce
1 tsp. Dijon mustard
2 Tbs. ketchup
4 green onions, chopped
3 Tbs. Dried parsley

2 tsp. Sesame oil
1 Tbs. Canola oil

1 Tbs. Cornstarch
¼ cup sugar
2 Tbs. Soy sauce
2 Tbs. Ketchup
¼ cup red wine vinegar
½ cup chicken broth
1 tsp. Hot sauce

2 Tbs. Chopped fresh cilantro

Combine first eight ingredients and shape into 5-6 patties. Set aside. In saucepan, combine the cornstarch, sugar, soy sauce, ketchup, vinegar, broth and hot sauce over medium heat until cornstarch is combined and the sauce has thickened and has a sheen to it. Remove from heat and add cilantro. Heat skillet to medium high, adding oils. Sauté salmon patties until brown on each side, about 4 minutes per side. Serve with Sweet Hot Sauce. Serves 5-6.

Sweet and Sour Chicken

1 Tbs. Cornstarch
¼ cup sugar
2 Tbs. Soy sauce
3 Tbs. Ketchup
¼ cup red wine vinegar
½ cup chicken broth

Combine above ingredients in a lidded jar and shake until combined. Set aside.

1 red onion, chopped finely
2 cloves garlic, pressed
1 tsp. Sesame oil
2 Tsp. Canola oil
4 boneless, skinless chicken breast halves, cut into one inch cubes
1 red bell pepper, cut into strips
¾ cup sugar snap peas
½ cup chopped carrots

In wok, or non stick skillet, sauté onions and garlic on medium high heat in oils until onions are transparent. Add chicken, peppers, peas and carrots and cook until chicken is no longer pink, about 8 minutes. Add sauce to mixture and cook through until sauce thickens, about two minutes. Serve with sticky rice. Serves 4-6. You can also make this dish with scallops. Yum!

Beef Stew

This is a particularly wonderful stew to concoct for a crock-pot. That way, the stew warms the house with its aroma. To prepare the stew for company, ladle stew into individual oven proof bowls, top with puff pastry and cook until pastry is browned, 12-15 minutes at 400 degrees. Call it stew en croute!

1 Tbs. butter
1 Tbs. olive oil
1 medium yellow onion, chopped
1 ½ pounds beef chuck, cubed into 1 ½ inch cubes
2 cloves garlic, pressed
2 Tbs. all purpose flour
1 tsp. sea salt
1 tsp. freshly ground pepper
2 cups carrots, peeled and cut into ½ inch dice
5 medium red potatoes, cubed
¼ cup chopped Italian parsley (or 3 Tbs. Dried)
1 Tbs. Dijon mustard
3 Tbs. jetchup
1 cup red wine
1 ¼ cup beef broth
3 Tbs. red wine vinegar

In large nonstick skillet, sauté onions over medium heat until caramelized (browning). Add beef and brown on all sides. Add garlic, flour, salt and pepper and stir through. Remove from heat. In a large crock- pot or stew pot, add carrots, potatoes, parsley and meat mixture. Combine mustard, ketchup, red wine, broth and vinegar in a small bowl and whisk until well mixed. Pour over stew. Let simmer all day over very low heat. Serves four very hungry people, or an average-sized family.

Marinated Flank Steak Over Open Flame

I find the simplest things taste the best. This easy marinade works well for all red meat, particularly steaks and kabobs.

1-2 pound flank steak
1 Tbs. Montreal steak seasoning*
5 Tbs. soy sauce
¼ cup red wine

Place flank steak and marinade in zippered plastic bag. Marinate all day. Heat grill to medium high. Cook 5-8 minutes per side until middle is pink, not red. Slice vertically at a 45-degree angle very thinly. An electric knife slices a flank very nicely. Serve with roasted potatoes and a tossed green salad.

*You can find Montreal steak seasoning at most grocery stores in the spice aisle. This spice is the best thing you can find to season a steak.

Note: If you would like to make kabobs, be sure to marinate the cubed red meat separately from the veggies. I like to marinate zucchini, yellow squash, red peppers and red onions in any store bought Italian dressing. Alternate meat and vegetables on a metal or soaked wooden skewer and place on the grill immediately. These take very little time to cook, so have your turning tongs and your serving platter handy.

Another Meat to Try: Our favorite cut of steak is tri-tip. Beef tri-tip is a boneless cut of meat from the bottom sirloin. It also is called "triangular" roast because of its shape. Most grocery stores on the west coast have it. If you can't find it, ask your butcher to cut it for you. This well marbled and very flavorful beef cut has been one of the beef industry's best-kept secrets. It's cheaper and tenderer than a New York cut. Marinate the tri-tip in the above marinade and grill on high, about 3-5 minutes per side for medium rare.

Homemade Taquitos

The first time I tasted homemade taquitos, I was hooked. It takes a bit of prep time, but everyone will enjoy your effort. Serve alongside homemade salsa, guacamole and Spanish rice. Makes 24 taquitos.

1 ½ cup leftover beef brisket, or chuck roast, shredded (You can also use rotisserie chicken)
1 can refried beans
1 Tbs. dried cumin
¼ cup salsa
1 small can green mild chilies
1 cup grated cheddar cheese
½ cup chopped onion (See note, page…)
24 corn tortillas
2 cups peanut oil

Combine meat, beans, cumin, salsa, chilies, cheese, and onion in food processor until it has the consistency of peanut butter, about one minute. Heat oil in deep frying pan to medium high heat. One by one, drop corn tortillas into oil and remove quickly. (This makes them easier to handle and roll.) Stack on paper towel-laden plate. When cool, press the tortillas down, squeezing extra oil back into frying pan, remembering to turn off the heat.

Spread a heaping tablespoon of bean mixture over the middle half of corn tortilla. Roll up and place seam side down on cookie sheet until all taquitos are rolled. Heat oil to medium high again. Place eight rolled tortillas, seam side down in hot oil. With tongs, turn taquitos over after 2-3 minutes, making sure they have browned. When both sides are finished, place on cookie sheet in a warm oven (325 degrees) and cook next two batches.

Piroshki's

These little pies are great for lunches the next day. Serve with mustard, ketchup, steak sauce or ranch dressing for dipping. If the idea of making a crust scares you, purchase ready-made piecrusts and divide into twelve equal parts. Press each into a circle and fill with meat mixture.

2 cups flour
1 tsp. Salt
2/3 cup vegetable shortening
7—9 Tbs. Very cold water

Combine flour, salt and shortening in bowl with pastry blender or two knives until mixture looks like little peas. Stirring with wooden spoon, add water one tablespoon at a time until dough is moistened and pliable. Form into a ball and let rest in the fridge, 30 minutes.

1 yellow onion, chopped finely
1 Tbs. Olive oil
3 cloves garlic, pressed
1 pound ground beef
2 cups shredded cabbage (cut like you would to make coleslaw)
1 large cooked and peeled potato, diced
¼ tsp. Salt
¼ tsp. pepper
¼ cup sour cream
1 tsp. Dried dill weed
1 tsp. Paprika

Sauté onion, garlic and meat until meat is thoroughly cooked, about ten minutes. Stir in cabbage and cook until wilted, another ten minutes. Remove from heat and stir in remaining ingredients.

To assemble: divide dough into twelve parts. Roll each portion into a six-inch circle. Spoon ¼ cup filling into center. Pull dough over itself, making the circle a half circle. Seal edges by pressing on them with fork tines. Pierce with three vent holes.

1 beaten egg yolk.

When finished, place Piroski's on greased cookie sheet and brush with egg yolk. Bake at 375 for 25-30 minutes until golden brown. Makes 12.

Stuffed Cabbage Roll Ups

This is a pretty labor intensive dish, but one that everyone loves. If you prepare the rice and cabbage beforehand, assembly is pretty quick.

1 ½ cup Japanese sticky rice
2-¼ cup water

In medium saucepan, bring rice and water to a boil. Reduce heat to low and cover twenty minutes. In the meantime. . .

Heat a large pot of water to boiling. Core one large cabbage by cutting out the stem end. Being careful not to tear the leaves, place leaves in batches of eight into boiling water. Cook three minutes until wilted. Place on plate and continue until all the cabbage is cooked.

1 tsp. olive oil
1 red onion, chopped*
3 cloves garlic, pressed
Salt and pepper to taste
1 pound ground beef
1 cup purchased spaghetti sauce
1 cup shredded mozzarella

In a non-stick frying pan, sauté onion and garlic over medium heat. Add salt, pepper and ground beef and cook until done, ten minutes. Remove from heat and add spaghetti sauce and mozzarella. When rice is done, stir into meat mixture.

Place ¼ cup of meat mixture in each cabbage leaf, pulling the ends together like a package and placing it seam side down in a greased 9x13 pan. Top the entire entourage with:

1 cup purchased spaghetti sauce
½ cup grated Swiss cheese

Bake at 350 for thirty minutes. Serves 6.

Beef Burritos

This is a new DeMuth family favorite, a meal in one handy package. Feel free to add any other ingredients.

2 cups Jasmine rice
3 cups water

Bring rice and water to a boil over high heat. Reduce to low, cover, and let simmer twenty minutes. Remove from heat.

1 can black beans
1 Tbs. taco seasoning
1 small can green chilies
½ cup salsa

In small saucepan over low heat, combine beans, seasoning, chilies and salsa. Keep warm until burritos are ready to assemble

½ to 1 pound leftover steak, cut in thin strips
½ tsp. Montreal steak seasoning
1 tsp. olive oil

In a non-stick frying pan, sauté the leftover steak strips in olive oil and seasoning until just heated.

10, 12-inch flour tortillas
Scant tablespoon peanut oil

On a non-stick frying pan or grill, heat tortillas in peanut oil until just barely browned.

1 cup grated pepper jack cheese
1 cup grated cheddar cheese
Sour cream and salsa

Ranch dressing (or use recipe for Cilantro Ranch on page 34)

To assemble, place all ingredients in cozy bowls along a sideboard (rice, beans, steak, cheeses, sour cream, salsa, and ranch dressing.) Starting with a healthy helping of rice, add beans, meat, cheese, sour cream and salsa. Fold ends in and roll, creating a pocketed burrito. Serves 5 hungry souls.

Marinade for Pork

This is similar to Chinese barbecued pork.

¼ cup olive oil
¼ cup ketchup
¼ cup red wine vinegar
2 Tbs. soy sauce
¼ cup brown sugar
Dash Worcestershire sauce
2 tsp. hot chili sauce
2 Tbs. steak sauce
½ cup chopped green onions
4 cloves pressed garlic

Marinate 2-3 pounds of pork tenderloins for 8-12 hours. Grill over medium heat, ten to twelve minutes a side, until inside is no longer pink. Slice into medallions and serve.

Pork Gyros

This recipe is an adaptation from a Greek favorite. It makes delicious use of leftover pork roast or pork chops.

4 pork chops or 1 pound leftover pork roast, cut into 1/8 inch slivers
½ cup white wine
2 cloves garlic, pressed
1 Tbs. Lemon juice
1 tsp. dried oregano
3 Tbs. olive oil
1 tsp. Cavendar's Greek Seasoning (available on the spice aisle of most grocery stores)

½ cup chopped tomatoes
¾ cup peeled and chopped cucumber
¼ cup red onion, minced
1 tsp. garlic powder
3 Tbs. Fresh oregano
¼ tsp. ground black pepper
1 cup plain yogurt
½ cup crumbled feta cheese

8 rounds pita bread
olive oil

Marinate pork strips in wine, garlic, lemon, oregano, olive oil and seasonings thirty minutes.

Combine tomatoes, cucumber, onion, garlic powder, oregano, pepper, yogurt and feta cheese. Set aside. Pour meat and marinade into non-stick pan and heat over medium high heat.

On griddle or non-stick pan, heat olive oil to medium high heat and cook both sides of pita bread. To serve, spoon pork into pita's center, top with feta mixture and fold over, like you would a taco. Serve with fruit salad. Serves four.

Mary's Meatloaf

The ultimate comfort food, this meatloaf is flavorful and easy to make. Serve with garlic mashed potatoes and corn on the cob.

1 ½ pound ground chuck
¼ cup chopped green onions
3 Tbs. ketchup
1 Tbs. Dijon mustard
1/2 cup bread crumbs
1 egg
1 Tbs. soy sauce
1 Tbs. dried parsley
½ tsp. dried oregano
2 Tbs. white wine
1 tsp. garlic powder
¼ tsp. black pepper
¼ tsp. salt

Preheat oven to 350. Mix all the ingredients together with your hands. (Yes, your hands!) Press into an un-greased loaf pan. Bake for 45-50 minutes until browned. Serves 4-6.

Clay Pot Ginger Chicken

Clay pot cooking renders the most tender roast chicken.

1 whole fryer, fat and giblets removed
¼ cup sesame oil
3 Tbs. oyster sauce
1 Tbs. Fresh ginger, minced finely
3 cloves garlic, pressed
½ cup chopped green onions
3 Tbs. sugar
¼ cup white wine
¼ cup soy sauce

In plastic gallon-sized zipper locked bag, combine oil, oyster sauce, ginger, garlic, green onions, sugar, wine and soy sauce. Place whole chicken inside and let marinate 2—8 hours.

Place large lidded clay pot (not glazed clay pot, but a specific cooking pot like Romertopf) in clean kitchen sink. Cover with water and let soak twenty minutes. Remove from water. Place chicken breast side up in clay pot. Pour marinade over and cover. Place clay pot in a cold oven. Turn oven on to 450 degrees. Bake for an hour and fifteen minutes until chicken is baked thoroughly and is nicely browned. Serve alongside stir-fried veggies and basmati rice. Serves 4.

If you don't have a clay pot, you can use a heavy lidded casserole dish. Bake at 400 degrees for 1 hour fifteen minutes.

Tartiflette

We had this in Southern France. It's easy to make and sooooo yummy.

6-8 medium red potatoes or yukon golds
1 package bacon, cut into small pieces
1 yellow onion 1 Tbs. butter
1/4 cup heavy cream
1 1/2 cups white wine
Strong white cheese, (In France they use Reblochon. You can try muenster, jack or Swiss cheese) 8-16 ounces, cut into thick pieces

Boil potatoes until tender. Cool slightly so they don't burn you when you cut them. Cut into thick rounds. Chop onion. Sauté in butter until translucent. Add bacon. Cook until bacon fat is rendered and onions begin to brown. Butter a large 9x13 pan. Put half of the potatoes on the bottom. Be sure to salt and pepper each layer of potatoes. Top with half the onion mixture Repeat for last layer. Pour wine and cream over the top. Place slabs of cheese over the top until the potatoes and onions are completely covered. Bake at 400 degrees for 20 minutes until heated through.

Italian Polenta Casserole

2 ½ cups chicken broth
3 Tbsp. butter
2 cups milk
1 ½ cups polenta
1 3oz. pkg. cream cheese, cut up
1 ½ cups purchased pasta sauce
5 oz. sliced hard salami, cut into strips
1 cup shredded mozzarella cheese (4 oz.)
½ cup finely shredded or grated parmesan cheese

In a large saucepan bring chicken broth and butter to boiling. Meanwhile, stir together the milk and polenta. Add polenta mixture to boiling broth. Cook and stir until bubbly; cook and stir about 5 minutes more or until thickened. Remove from heat. Stir in cream cheese until well mixed. Spread in a buttered 13x9x2 inch baking pan. If desired, cover and chill up to 24 hours.

Preheat oven to 375 degrees. Pour pasta sauce over polenta layer. Sprinkle with salami and cheeses. Bake, uncovered, for 30 minutes or until heated through. Makes 6 to 8 servings.

Fish Tacos

4 tilapias filets cut into 1 x 4 inch sticks

Mix together:
½ cup cornstarch
¼ tsp. salt and pepper
½ tsp. Old Bay Seasoning

1 ½ cups julienned cabbage (either red, white or napa, or a combination of all three).
1 cup cilantro ranch dressing (see page 34)

10-15 corn tortillas
corn oil

Dredge tilapia filets in cornstarch mixture. Then place them in a frying pan that has about an inch of peanut oil, already hot. Fish should make a sizzling noise when you put it in. Fry until done on both sides, about 5 minutes. Drain fish on paper towels.

Mix cabbage and ranch and place in a bowl.

Saute corn tortillas in corn oil either in a skillet or grill. Drain on paper towels. Be sure not to overcook (where they start turning brown) or they'll be too stiff to use.

Serve tacos with cabbage mixture and cut limes.

Chapter 7
VEGGIES

If you want to lose weight, be sure you're eating meat the size of a deck of cards. Limit your intake of fruit. And eat one million veggies. Vegetables are the safest foods known to man, but most of the time they take second fiddle to the meat or starch we cook. To bring better health to your home and table, choose to think of vegetables as the star on your plate, and offer more than one veggie choice as a side.

Consider planting a garden this year, even if that means growing some patio tomatoes in pots on the back deck. Fresh from the ground is always the best way to eat vegetables as they retain their flavor and burst with vitamins. If gardening scares you, look for a local farm that has a CSA (farm share). We belong to one, and it's been a huge blessing. We pay a set fee per year, then every other week we pick up our share of fresh vegetables. I've learned to cook things I've never cooked before, and we've had the privilege of eating organic veggies.

Minted Carrots

4 large carrots, peeled and cut into three inch sticks
1/4 cup chicken stock (You can use bouillon for any of these recipes…. I use a chicken food base)
1 tsp. butter
1/2 tsp. sugar
1/2 tsp. dried mint (or 2 teaspoons fresh)
2 tsp. white wine

Place the carrots sticks into a microwave proof dish with the stock. Place plastic wrap over and cook on high for three minutes. Place carrots in a frying pan with the butter just melted. Saute for one minute. Add sugar, mint, wine, and 1/4 cup of the remaining stock. Bring to a boil. Serve immediately.

Balsamic Green Beans

4 cups steamed green beans
1 red bell pepper, julienned and steamed with beans
1/4 cup olive oil
1 tsp. garlic powder
3 Tbs. balsamic vinegar
3 Tbs. brown sugar
1 tsp. fresh oregano
1/2 cup feta cheese

Combine olive oil, vinegar, sugar, garlic powder and oregano in dressing container and shake well. Pour over hot bean and pepper mixture. Crumble feta cheese over the top, and toss. Serves 4-6.

Grilled Summer Squash

1 zucchini (about ten inches long)
1 yellow summer squash (looks like a yellow zucchini) 10 inches long
4 Tbs. olive oil
2 Tbs. balsamic vinegar
1 tsp. kosher sea salt
ground pepper to taste
2 cloves garlic, pressed
3 Tbs. chopped fresh basil

Slice squash lengthwise, making 1/4 inch thick slabs. Combine marinade in shallow baking dish. Toss with the squash. Refrigerate 4-6 hours.

Heat grill to medium high, and put squash on as if you would put a steak on the grill. Turn when starting to brown. Make sure the squash becomes translucent, and that it has grill lines. Return to marinade and keep warm in a 200 degree oven until ready to serve. Serves 4.

Purple Hull Peas the Only Way

Purple Hull Peas are a Texas treat. Get them fresh in the springtime, or use black eyed peas (fresh).

5 slices bacon, diced
½ yellow onion, chopped
1 clove garlic, pressed
2 cups purple hull peas
5 cups chicken broth

Saute bacon, onion and garlic until cooked through. Add fresh peas. Cover with chicken broth and bring to a boil. Turn the heat down to low and cover the peas. Cook one hour until tender.

These are served best with a side of ranch dressing.

Roasted Asparagus

(or any veggie, really. You can use broccoli, cauliflower, squash...)

Toss 24 spears of asparagus with:

3 Tbs extra virgin olive oil
Sea salt and pepper to taste
1 tsp. granulated garlic

Roast at 400 degrees for 15 minutes. Stir occasionally.

The Best Creamed Corn with a kick

¼ cup chopped green onions
½ cup chopped red bell pepper
2 Tbs. butter
4 cups frozen corn
2 small cans green chiles
1 8-ounce package cream cheese
½ cup milk
Salt and pepper to taste

In a large skillet, saute green onions and bell peppers in butter until just starting to brown. Add corn and cook until corn starts browning (this gives it smokier flavor). Add chiles and cream cheese and cook over medium heat until cream cheese starts melting into the corn. It will be very thick. Thin with milk until the mixture has a creamy, spoonable consistency. Add salt and pepper. Serves 6.

Caramelized carrots

8 large carrots, peeled and sliced into 4-inch sticks
2 Tbs. butter
4 Tbs. brown sugar
1 Tbs. maple syrup

Sauté the carrots in butter until they start to brown. Add brown sugar and maple syrup and cook until the liquid mixture caramelizes. Serves 5.

Chapter 8
DRINKS

I never knew about iced tea, or appreciated it until I moved to Texas. The first sweet tea I had made me gag. To me, it tasted like flat Coke. Way too sweet. But over the years, the drink confection has grown on me to the point that I now mix half sweet tea (It's never called iced tea here, just tea), half unsweet tea.

And because I live in Texas, I've learned to concoct some yummy cold drinks. There's nothing so refreshing as an iced beverage on a 100+ degree sweltering day.

But those of you reading this cookbook in winter, don't despair. There's always Italian hot chocolate, my all time favorite winter beverage that borders more on pudding than drink. I first had it in Italy, and I've been hooked ever since.

Semi-Sweet Herbal Iced Tea

8 tea bags (Our family likes any infusion of green tea, cranberries, or pomegranate. If you use a berry tea, the tea turns a great shade of fuchsia!)
¾ cup sugar
4 cups water

Boil tea bags and sugar until tea is rendered. Remove tea bags. Pour liquid into 1 gallon pitcher. Add ice cubes and water until the pitcher is full. To the entire mix add:

3 Tbs. lemon juice (I use the concentrate kind.)

Yogurt Smoothie

1 1/2 cups nonfat plain yogurt (buy the big tubs of this for cheaper)
1 handful of frozen mixed berries
1 frozen banana, diced

Throw in a blender and blend. It's filling and yummy!

Italian Hot Chocolate

We all fell in love with this in Italy. It's like drinking a thin, rich pudding. Trust me, you'll never go back to powdered after this.

½ cup unsweetened cocoa
½ cup white sugar
1 tsp. cornstarch
2 cups milk

Mix together the dry ingredients. Add milk to a saucepan and heat until just below boiling. Whisk in the dry ingredients and keep whisking as the mixture thickens. It can burn easily, so keep stirring, and turn down the heat if it gets really bubbly. Once it's thickened, it's ready to serve. This is really dense and rich, so it makes 4 servings in demitasse cups. Top with whipped cream and chocolate shavings.

The Best Punch Ever

1 2-liter bottle ginger ale
1 can frozen cranberry juice concentrate
1 can water
½ cup frozen raspberries

Combine and serve!

Hot Spiced Apple Cider

1 can frozen apple juice concentrate
3 cans full of water
¼ cup brown sugar
2 tsp. cinnamon
dash of cloves, allspice, and nutmeg

Combine all ingredients on the stove top and heat until warm. Serve with cinnamon sticks.

Homemade Lemonade

1 cup sugar
1 cup water

Heat on stove until sugar dissolves and is thickened. This is called a simple syrup.

5 lemons, juiced.

In half gallon pitcher add the juice from 5 lemons (and you can throw in the discarded halves), the simple syrup, and ice cubes and water to fill it.

Chapter 9
BREADS

"He told them still another parable: 'The kingdom of heaven is like yeast that a woman took and mixed into a large amount of flour until it worked all through the dough." Matthew 13:33

My husband jokes that my first loaf of bread could be used to build a brick fireplace, it was so hard. Still, he ate it—chewing and chewing until he dutifully swallowed the mealy lump. For years, bread-making was an elusive art, something mastered only by folks wearing tall white hats. Me? Well, I made bricks.

It wasn't until Eva came into our lives that I understood what I was doing wrong. For the month after our second child was born, Eva cleaned, entertained my oldest, let me nap, and made amazing bread. She taught me that I needed to "proof" the yeast—let it sit in a warm, sweet liquid until it bubbled. She gently told me I was under-kneading. She showed me how to beat and push the dough into submission for fifteen minutes.

"See here? It needs to feel like this." She gave the dough a good spank. "You need to work the yeast and gluten all the way through the dough until it's no longer tough, but stretchy."

Thanks to Eva, I now make high rising bread, and my husband no longer has to chew until his teeth hurt.

I realized my bread-making journey is a lot like spiritual growth.

We need tenacity. It took me four years to perfect my first loaf of bread. Growing in Christ requires a similar endurance. Upon failing, we need to go forward even if we're discouraged or disheartened.

105

We need to knead longer. So much of life is convenience and instantaneous gratification. If we expect this in our spiritual life, the end result will be dry, hard spirituality. We need to allow the Bread of Life to knead His gluten and yeast into our hearts. His kneading hurts, but it yields high-rising spirituality and hearts that stretch.

We need mentors. I didn't understand how well-kneaded dough was supposed to feel. I needed the expertise of someone who understood bread-making, and I needed to be humble enough to accept her help. God places mentors in our lives to show us how to live and to encourage us as we struggle.

Whole-wheat Corn Bread

2 eggs
1 cup milk
1/3 cup sugar
1/4 cup oil
1/4 tsp. salt
1 cup corn meal
3/4 cup wheat flour
1 Tbs. baking powder

Mix eggs, milk, sugar, oil, and salt in medium bowl. Combine flour, corn meal and baking powder in large mixing cup. Pour into wet mixture and whisk until smooth. Pour in 9x11 greased pan. Bake at 400 degrees for 25 minutes or until a toothpick poked in the middle comes out clean.

Serve with honey butter:

1/4 cup butter, softened
7 Tbs. honey

Whisk together and serve with a spoon.

Italian Dinner Rolls

1 ¼ cup very warm water (not boiling—just hot tap water)
1 tbs. active dry yeast
1 tbs. malt powder*
1 tbs. high gluten flour*

¼ cup powdered milk
¼ cup softened butter
¼ cup sugar
1 egg
1 tsp. kosher salt
5 cups bread flour

½ cup melted butter
1 Tbs. garlic powder
1 Tbs. dried parsley flakes

In large see-though measuring cup, combine water, yeast, malt powder and high gluten flour. Let sit ten minutes until bubbly.

In large bowl of a stand mixer, add powdered milk, softened butter, sugar, egg, salt, yeast mixture and four cups flour. Using a dough hook, turn on low speed and add flour until dough is no longer sticky. Turn to medium and knead 7-10 minutes. (If you don't have a stand mixer or a food processor with a dough blade, combine ingredients in large bowl and hand knead fifteen minutes. You can also add the ingredients in order into a bread machine and use the dough setting only.)

Pull dough out. Spray bowl with cooking spray and return dough to bowl. Cover with plastic wrap and let rise one hour. Punch down. Using about ¼ to ½ cup of dough at a time, roll into a thick 6 inch snake. Loop the dough around, pulling one end through, like you are tying a knot. (Or if you prefer, shape into a ball.)

Place rolls on a greased cookie sheet. Let rise one hour. Bake at 375 for 15—20 minutes until the tops are golden brown.

Microwave butter in large mug for thirty seconds until melted. Add garlic powder and parsley and stir through. With a large pastry brush, brush the tops of each roll with the butter mixture. Makes 24—28 rolls.

*You can purchase malt flour and high gluten flour at most specialty food markets, or order them from the Baker's Catalog. Web site: www.kingarthurflour.com or call toll free 800.827.6836.

Kitchen Tip: If you decide to make bread on a regular basis, buy a large package of yeast at a warehouse club (usually less than five dollars). Pour yeast (about 2 cups) in gallon sized zipper bag and store in the freezer for long-term use. This greatly reduces your cost in bread-making.

Cheddar Biscuits

Another great addition is 1/4 cup chopped chives and/or crumbled bacon. Adding ¼ tsp. ground black pepper gives this a kick if you're up for it!

2 cups all purpose flour, or bread flour
2 1/2 tsp. baking powder
1/4 tsp. salt
1/2 tsp. baking soda
1 tsp. sugar
1/4 tsp. paprika
1 tsp. dried dill
1/3 cup butter or margarine
1 cup loosely packed grated cheddar cheese
3/4 cup milk with 1 Tbs. white wine vinegar added (makes mock buttermilk)

In a medium bowl, stir together first seven ingredients. Cut the butter into the flour mixture until the mixture resembles fine crumbs. Add cheddar cheese and distribute evenly into the mixture. Add "buttermilk" to mixture and stir until a ball forms. Knead dough on a floured surface, only kneading ten times (or it will get tough.) With a floured rolling pin, roll the dough to a one inch thickness. Cut circles into the dough with a circular cookie cutter, until all dough is used. Place biscuits nearly touching on a buttered baking sheet. Bake in a preheated oven at 400 degrees for 15-20 minutes until brown. Makes 12-15 biscuits.

Easy Italian crusty/chewy bread (No Kneading!)

This is the yummiest and easiest bread.

2 cups tepid water plus 1 tablespoon
1 tsp dry active yeast
1 tsp salt
4 cups all-purpose flour

Add the water, yeast, salt, and flour into a mixing bowl. Using a spatula or wooden spoon, stir well to form a wet, very sticky dough. Do not try to knead with your hands, as it is too sticky to handle. Once mixed, cover the bowl with a towel, and leave out at room temperature for 24 hours.

Preheat oven to 450. Place Dutch oven, or other oven proof, lidded pot in the oven. Let it heat up with the oven until it's very hot. Open oven and take off lid. Spray interior of pot with cooking spray, then ladle out the sticky dough with a spatula into the Dutch oven. Cover. Lower oven temperature to 400 degrees. Bake for 25 minutes. Remove cover. Bake for 35 additional minutes until golden brown. This recipe is easily doubled.

Country Wheat Bread

1 ¼ cup warm water
1 Tbs. yeast
1 tsp. sugar
1 Tbs. flour

Combine and let sit until the mixture gets bubbly, about 5 minutes. Drop into bowl, then add:

3 cups white flour
1 cup+ whole wheat flour. (You can make this 50/50 or with 100% whole wheat flour if you want a more dense bread. King Arthur Flour makes a white 100% whole wheat flour.)
1/3 cup softened or melted butter
1 egg
1/4 cup honey
2 Tbs. molasses
¼ cup brown sugar
¼ cup powdered milk
½ tsp. salt

Place in greased bowl and let rise one hour. Punch down. Form into two long loaves; let rise one hour. Bake at 350 for 30 minutes until golden brown.

Quick Wheat Bread with a Kick

1 cup wheat flour
2 cups white flour
1/4 cup honey
1 tsp. salt
4 tsp. baking powder
1 cup light-colored beer
1/2 cup milk

Throw all ingredients in large bowl. Stir until combined. Pour into a greased loaf pan. Bake at 350 for one hour. Simple!

To make cheese bread:

Omit wheat flour (3 cups white instead)
Add 1 cup grated cheddar cheese

French Bread

1 ¼ cup very warm water
1 Tbs. malt flour
1 Tbs. high gluten flour
2 Tbs. dry active yeast

Let stand five minutes until bubbly. Pour into mixing bowl.

To mixing bowl add
1 tsp. lemon juice
1 Tbs. sugar
1 cup semolina flour
¼ cup olive oil
1 tsp. Sea salt
3—3-1/2 cups white bread flour

Mix until elastic, not sticky, like you can spank it—ten minutes. Remove bread from bowl, spray bowl with cooking spray and return dough to bowl. Cover with plastic wrap and let rise one hour. Punch down and shape into loaves. Let rise one hour. Preheat oven to 450. Spray interior with water just before you put bread in. Place bread in oven. Spray again. Turn heat down to 400. Spray bread three times, every two minutes or so. This simulates a steam injected French oven. Total baking time 20-25 minutes. Cool on rack. Makes 2.

Basic White Bread

1 ¼ cup very warm water
1 Tbs. malt flour
1 Tbs. high gluten flour
2 Tbs. dry active yeast

Let stand five minutes until bubbly. Pour into mixing bowl.

To mixing bowl add:

1/4 cup butter
1 tsp. sea salt
¼ cup dry milk powder
¼ cup sugar
1 egg
5 cups bread flour

Mix until elastic, not sticky, like you can spank it—ten minutes. Remove bread from bowl, spray bowl with cooking spray and return dough to bowl. Cover with plastic wrap and let rise one hour. Punch down and shape into loaves. Let rise one hour. This is also really good as dinner rolls. Preheat oven to 375 and bake 25-30 minutes until golden brown.

If making rolls, melt ½ cup butter. To that add 1 Tbs. Garlic powder and 1 Tbs. Parsley. When rolls are done (they take 15-20 minutes), brush their tops with butter mixture. You can also add parmesan to the butter mixture.

Zucchini Bread

3 eggs
1 cup brown sugar
1 cup white sugar
1 cup oil
2 cups shredded zucchini
1 tsp. vanilla
2 cups flour
2 tsp. baking soda
¼ tsp. baking powder
1/4 tsp. salt
1 Tbs. cinnamon (Yes, a tablespoon. Trust me.)

Combine eggs, sugars, oil, zucchini and vanilla in stand mixture until smooth. Stir soda, powder, salt and cinnamon into flour. Pour flour into wet mixture and mix over low speed until well combined. Pour into two 9x5 greased loaf pans. Bake at 350 for one hour.

Pumpkin Wheat Bread

3 eggs
1 cup brown sugar
3/4 cup white sugar
1 cup oil
1 ½ cups pureed pumpkin
1 tsp. vanilla
1 1/2 cups all purpose flour
½ cup whole wheat flour
2 tsp. baking soda
¼ tsp. baking powder
1/4 tsp. salt
1 Tbs. cinnamon

Combine eggs, sugars, oil, pumpkin and vanilla in stand mixture until smooth. Stir soda, powder, salt and cinnamon into flours. Pour flour into wet mixture and mix over low speed until well combined. Pour into two 9x5 greased loaf pans. Bake at 350 for one hour

Chapter 10
DESSERTS

Dessert leaves a sweet taste in your guests' mouths before they leave. Sweets are the icing on the cake of your entertaining. I've found that the simplest desserts are often the best loved and most remembered.

By far, my husband Patrick is the dessert chef in our family. He makes the best crème brulee, and he's not afraid to try tricky meringues and soufflés. Me? I tend toward chocolate, chocolate, chocolate. But I've thrown in a few other of our favorites, a new one being the grilled pound cake (oh my).

Truffles

2 cups semi-sweet chocolate chips
1/4 cup heavy whipping cream
2 Tbs. salted butter
1/2 cup powdered sugar
1 Tbs. vanilla extract
Bakers cocoa powder

Place all ingredients in a microwave proof bowl. Place bowl in microwave on high for thirty seconds. Take it out and stir thoroughly. Place it back in for thirty additional seconds. Stir.

Do this until mixture is completely melted. Cool mixture in refrigerator until it is relatively hard. With a teaspoon, scoop out a ball. Roll it in your hands until it is perfectly round. When you have rolled all the balls (about thirty), roll them in bakers cocoa powder (non-sweetened). Keep refrigerated. Serve in little paper or foil cups.

Espresso Brownies

Do you see a chocolate trend here?

Who can resist coffee and chocolate morphed together in a brownie? I developed these several years ago as a use for my hubby's leftover espresso. The brownies have no leavening other than eggs, so they're decadent and rich.

3/4 cup cocoa powder (the baking kind, no sweetening)
1/2 cup old coffee or espresso
3/4 cup butter (yep! so fattening!)

Microwave the above in a glass measuring cup for 30 second intervals (stir between) until butter is melted. Pour into a mixing bowl. Add:

1 1/2 cups sugar
3 eggs
1 tsp. vanilla
1 cup all purpose flour
1 cup chopped nuts (optional)

Spread into a greased 9 x 13 pan. Bake for 30-35 minutes at 350 degrees.

Pears a la Mary

5 pears, halved, cored and peeled
3 Tbs. butter
5 Tbs. raspberry jam
3/4 cup chocolate chips
3 Tbs. powdered sugar
1 tsp. vanilla
2 Tbs. butter
1/4 cup heavy cream

slivered almonds for garnish

Sauté pears in butter in non-stick pan until they are browned. In the meantime, spread a dollop of raspberry jam in a 5 inch circle on a dessert plate. Place chocolate, powdered sugar, vanilla, butter and cream in microwavable container. Microwave on high for 30 seconds. Stir. Microwave 30 more seconds. Stir. Repeat until melted through. Place two pear halves on top of jammed plates. Drizzle chocolate over. Top with nuts.

Java Mint Brownies

¾ cup cocoa powder
½ cup coffee
¾ cup butter

1 1/2 cups sugar
3 eggs
1 tsp. peppermint extract
1 cup all purpose flour

3 extra large packages Junior Mints

Preheat oven to 350. Microwave the first three ingredients in a large microwave safe bowl for thirty seconds, or until butter is melted. Stir until combined. Add next five ingredients, and stir with wooden spoon until just combined. Spread into a greased 9x13 glass pan and bake for 35 minutes.

Let cool.

Microwave Junior Mints in glass bowl for thirty seconds. Stir. Microwave again for thirty seconds. Stir. Repeat until mint mixture is fully melted and is easily pourable. Pour onto cooled brownies. Spread evenly. Serve with vanilla bean ice cream. Makes 12.

SIDE NOTE: I discovered this icing by accident. My friends John and Donna brought us several boxes of Junior mints, but they melted in the car into a Junior Mint blob. So, I thought I'd see what kind of icing they would make melted. The result? Amazing! It just goes to show you can take something ruined and make it remarkable with a little creativity.

Also, these brownies are delicious without the icing. If you're not a mint fan, omit the Junior Mint icing and enjoy!

Mary's Chocolate Oatmeal Cookies

1 ½ cup thick cut oatmeal
¾ cup all purpose flour
½ tsp. baking soda
6 Tbs. baking cocoa
1 stick butter (1/2 cup)
½ cup light brown sugar
½ cup white sugar
1 egg
1 tsp. vanilla

Stir together the first four ingredients, set aside. In bowl, cream together the butter, sugars, egg and vanilla. Stir the dry ingredients into the sugar mixture. Drop by tablespoon onto lightly greased cookie sheet. Bake at 350 for ten minutes.

Pound Cake Layered with Raspberries

1 large pound cake (found in frozen food section of grocery store)
1 ½ package Neufchatel cream cheese
¾ cup powdered sugar
1 tsp. vanilla
3 Tbs. butter, softened
½ cup Nutella
2 cups fresh raspberries

Using a serrated knife, cut the pound cake horizontally into four slices (3 cuts). Combine cream cheese, sugar, vanilla and butter in a stand mixer and mix until well combined. On each layer (except top) spread ½ of the Nutella, followed 1/3 of the cream cheese mixture and top with 1/3 of the berries. Do this for the two middle layers. On the top, spread the remaining 1/3 of the cream cheese mixture and top with remaining 1/3 raspberries. To serve, cut the cake vertically and place on dessert plate so the layers show. Top with whipped cream, if desired. Makes 6-8 servings.

Cranberry Bars

2 cups all purpose flour
½ tsp. baking soda
¼ tsp. salt
1 cup white sugar
2/3 cup melted butter
1 large egg
1 tsp. vanilla
¾ cup coarsely chopped macadamia nuts
¾ cup sweetened dried cranberries
¾ cup white chocolate chips

Sift flour, baking soda and salt. In stand mixer, mix sugar, butter, egg and vanilla until well combined. Add flour mixture. Fold in nuts, berries and chips. Spread onto a greased 9x13 pan. Bake at 325 degrees for 20-25 minutes until a toothpick inserted into the center comes out clean. Makes 24 bars.

Nutella Cookies

Oh how I love Nutella! I developed this recipe because of my sheer infatuation with it.

1/4 cup butter
1/4 cup cream cheese
1/2 cup Nutella
1/2 cup white sugar
1/2 cup brown sugar
1 egg
1/2 tsp. vanilla
1 1/4 cup flour mixed with 3/4 tsp. baking soda

Melt butter and cream cheese in microwave for thirty seconds on high until nearly melted. Add nutella, sugars, egg, and vanilla. Beat in flour and soda. Drop cookies onto ungreased baking sheet and cook at 375 for 10 minutes. Makes 3 dozen.

Chocolate Chocolate Chip Cookies:

1 cup melted butter
3/4 cup brown sugar
2/3 cup white sugar
2 eggs

1/4 cup cocoa powder (unsweetened)
3 cups flour
1/2 tsp salt
1 tsp baking soda
1 1/2 cup semi sweet chocolate chips

Combine dry ingredients and wet separately. Then combine together. Spoon onto greased cookie sheet. Bake at 325 for 12 minutes. So good!

Grilled Pound Cake with Berry Coulis

The simplest recipes are the best. We first had a variation of this at our favorite restaurant, Chiloso.

1 large pound cake (Sarah Lee can't be beat) sliced into 8 thick pieces.
½ stick softened butter

Butter both sides of pound cake, then grill them on a griddle until they're browned on both sides.

1 cup frozen berries (or you can use fresh)
½ cup white sugar
2 tsp. lemon juice
½ cup water

Place berries, sugar, lemon juice and water in small sauce pan and boil until cooked through. Using a hand blender, pulverize the mixture until it looks like a coulis (jamlike, but a little runnier).

To plate: Spread a large dollop of coulis on plate. Top with pound cake. If you're so inclined, add whipped cream.

Chocolate Ganache Cake

This is my go-to dessert when I want to impress someone with chocolate, chocolate, chocolate.

2 cups semi sweet chocolate chips
¾ cup butter
¾ cup powdered sugar
1 tablespoon flour
4 egg yolks
1 tsp. vanilla
4 egg whites
½ cup sour cream
½ cup plain yogurt

Melt chocolate and butter in 30 second increments in the microwave, stirring each time. Add to a mixing bowl. Add sugar, flour, egg yolks, and vanilla and mix through. In separate mixing bowl, add egg whites and mix until stiff peaks form. Gently fold egg whites into chocolate mixture. Spoon half of the chocolate mixture into a greased 12-inch round spring form pan.

Fold in sour cream and yogurt to the remaining chocolate, then gently spoon over the top of the darker chocolate mixture, being careful not to take it to the edges. You'll have a large circle of the lighter mixture in the middle of the darker mixture, leaving 1 inch of dark all the way around. This makes the darker mixture form a crust, and the lighter mixture becomes like cheesecake.

Bake at 375 degrees for thirty minutes. Let cool, then refrigerate, and serve cold. Serve with berries and whipped cream.

Simple But Elegant Pudding Dessert

1 package instant vanilla pudding
2 cups milk
Berries
Nutella
Store bought cookies

Whip milk and pudding together until thickened. Pour pudding into four bowls.

Top with berries, a dollop of Nutella, and 2 sugar cookies (or any other kind of cookie).

Peanut Butter Cupcakes with Ganache Frosting

¼ cup salted butter
½ cup peanut butter
2/3 cups packed brown sugar
1 egg
1 tsp. vanilla
2/3 cup milk
1 ¼ cup flour
½ Tbs. baking powder
¼ tsp. salt

Combine butter, peanut butter and brown sugar and mix until creamy. Add egg, vanilla and milk and stir through. Combine flour, baking powder and salt in a separate bowl, then add in batches to the wet ingredients.

Line a muffin tin with paper liners, and be sure to spray them too. (They'll be easier for your guests to take off the paper later.) Divide dough into twelve cups. Bake at 350 for 25 minutes.

1 cup semi sweet chocolate chips
1/3 cup heavy cream
½ tsp. vanilla

Place ingredients into large see-through measuring cup. Place in microwave for thirty seconds, then stir. Repeat until the ganache is fully melted. When cupcakes are cooled, pour the ganache over the top. Makes one dozen yummy cupcakes. You can also chop some peanuts and throw them on top if you wish.

Incredibly Easy Chocolate Shortbread

3/4 cup salted butter, softened
½ cup powdered sugar
¾ cup semi sweet chocolate chips
¼ cup butter (yes, more!)
2 cups flour

Mix together butter and sugar until smooth. Place chocolate chips and ¼ cup butter in glass bowl and microwave 30 seconds. Stir. Then microwave again for 30 seconds. Repeat until the chocolate is melted.

Combine butter mixture and chocolate mixture. Then add flour and stir through until well combined.

Spoon into a 9 x 13 baking dish that's been greased. Bake at 300 degrees for 40 minutes. Cut into bars. Eat, eat, eat.

ABOUT THE AUTHOR

Mary DeMuth is super fun, cute, and nice. She is an author extraordinaire and loves to cook like a queen. She has three beautiful children, Sophie the Super Fly, Aidan the Awesome, and Julia the Jubilant, and an adoring husband, Patrick the Perfect. Her hobbies include cooking (duh!), gardening, writing, dancing, underwater basket weaving, running, touching her toes, and knitting. Her greatest aspiration in life is to become a singing astronaut on Mars. Mary now lives in Texas with her family (aside from her way cool collegiate daughter) her dog, Pippin, her cat, Madeline, and a new kitty, Scout.

(Note: Sophie the Super Fly wrote this section. She's funny.)

Turn the page to see the folks who eat the lion's share of Mary's recipes:

Sophie, Aidan, Mary, Patrick and Julia. (And no, that's not their home.)

Find out more about Mary, her trove of books, and discovering impossible joy at MaryDeMuth.com.

Made in the USA
San Bernardino, CA
04 February 2013